E-MAILS FROM BAGHDAD

BY CAPTAIN TIMOTHY A. TATE
A PHOTOGRAPHIC JOURNAL OF BAGHDAD DURING OPERATION IRAQI FREEDOM II

*This book is dedicated to Dr. Greg Retallack (University of Oregon)
who believed in me, and Dr. Allan J. Busacca (Washington State University)
who pushed me harder to go farther than I ever could have gone alone.*

*This book represents the thoughts, ideas and opinions of Captain Timothy A.
Tate and in no way represents the U.S. military or government in any way or fashion.*

To order additional copies of this book, contact:
Xlibris
1-888-795-4274
www.Xlibris.com
Orders@Xlibris.com

ISBN: Softcover   978-1-4257-3801-3
        Hardcover   978-1-4257-3802-0
        EBook   978-1-7960-8779-6

Library of Congress Control Number: 2006909090

Print information available on the last page

Rev. date: 02/14/2020

PREFACE

I was asked to volunteer to go with a National Guard unit from my home state to serve in Iraq with Operation Iraqi Freedom II. I served with the 1st Cavalry Division in Baghdad, Iraq at their Division Headquarters near the airport in southwestern Baghdad.

During the first four and a half months I worked as one of the many night shift battle captains and monitored the battlefield during the height of the Mehdi militia and Falluja uprisings. I had the grizzly task of verifying information about the death of American soldiers and writing the initial three to four sentence press releases.

I also escorted and chauffeured members of the media.

I developed many opinions and had many insights into the military life and the operations in Iraq. I shared some of these carefully selected opinions and insights with my friends and family back home.

During those first four months on the night-shift, I became acquainted with the division Civil Affairs (G-5) section. I was able to get to know Lieutenant Colonel (LTC) Rick Welch who was in charge of Civil Affairs for the greater Baghdad area and his convoy detachment leader CPT Brian Ennesser.

I was invited to go out with them on missions. I took my personal cameras along for photographing the soldiers and Baghdad while we convoyed to various locations. I would share these pictures with the soldiers of the G-5 section and I soon became a popular fixture with the section.

First Cavalry Division's Civil Military Advisor, LTC Rick Welch's job was to represent the 1st Cavalry Division's Commanding General, Major General Peter Chiarelli, in establishing and maintaining relationships with highly influential people throughout Baghdad. In these meetings, which were conducted all over Baghdad, LTC Welch attempted to open doors of communication and establish relationships that could

potentially help the Coalition Forces successfully gain security and rebuild the infrastructure in and around Baghdad.

To get wherever he needed to go in Baghdad in order to meet with local leaders, LTC Welch relied on his Personal Security Detachment (PSD) led by CPT Brian Ennesser. The detachment was made

Captain Tim Tate inside a Blackhawk helicopter with the city of Baghdad reflecting in his glasses.

The Shadow Force, as they called their unit, was the personal security detachment for LTC Rick Welch who was the Division Civil Affairs Officer. From left to right, SPC Clark, Unknown, SGT Brown, SSG Moreno, SSG Mosqueda (up top), CPT Enneser, SSG Gray, SPC Fields and SSG Garcia.

The 1st Cavalry Division Civil Affairs Section from atop of one of the buildings by Z Lake, seen in the background. From left to right; SSG Mosqueda, SSG Moreno, CPT Woods; SSG Garcia; SSG Gray, SFC Stadtler, MAJ Castro, CPT Beunteo, MAJ Thorton, LTC Welch, MAJ Tzucanow, MAJ Lloyd, SGT Brown, MAJ Cole, SPC Fields, MSG Simmons.

up of active duty and reservist soldiers who volunteered to come together and run the three-Humvee convoy that was on call 24/7 to provide transportation for the colonel.

CPT Ennesser was an active duty captain who was recruited by LTC Welch to lead the detachment because of his 18 months of experience as an Opposition Forces commander at the Joint Readiness Training Center (JRTC). With a strong background in guerrilla warfare and operations involving civilians on the battlefield, CPT Ennesser was a logical choice.

The soldiers in the convoy decided that they needed a nickname like the other military units and called themselves the "Shadow Force."

CPT Ennesser bragged about the Shadow Force's ability to get the colonel anywhere he needed to be at any time ASAP! Once the colonel made a decision or

SGT Brown was one of the machinegunners for Shadow Force.

received a phone call, the Shadow Force was lined up and ready to roll within an hour and within another hour the colonel was in any part of Baghdad he wanted to be in. They usually got him to

the desired place in less than an hour.

The soldiers that formed the Shadow Force came together from many different directions. The bulk of the unit was made up of Texas

National Guardsman from various units, walks of life and from different parts of Texas.

SSG Moreno was an engineer and a factory manager at a company that operates plants on both sides of the Texas and Mexican border. He was able to volunteer for this mission because his company went the extra mile to support him during his tour of duty. He was one of the main machinegunners in the Shadow Force for the year-long deployment.

SSG Mosqueda was an assistant principal at White High School in Dallas, Texas. The school posted a huge photograph of SSG Mosqueda in the school cafeteria so everyone would remember him while he was serving in Baghdad.

SSG Frank Garcia (cover picture) worked as a full time maintenance technician for the Texas National Guard. SSG Garcia left his first newborn child to go to Vietnam and now, many

Above: LTC Rick Welch served as the 1st Cavalry Division Civil Affairs Officer for OIF II. Right: The Humvees in a convoy, July of 2004, after up armor kits were added. Note that the air conditioning units had not been added yet and were not added until after the summer months were over, sometime in the October and November time frame of 2004. Far Right: SSG Moreno prepares the machinegun prior to a convoy.

years later he had to leave his first newborn grandchild to go to Baghdad. According to SSG Garcia, it was more difficult for him to have to leave his new grandchild behind.

SPC Clarke, the only other active duty soldier who volunteered to be apart of Shadow Force, said he joined the unit to keep from spending the war behind a

desk working as a unit clerk. He became Colonel Welch's driver and radio operator.

By the time Shadow Force hit the ground in Baghdad, each member had memorized every highway and major section of the city of Baghdad. When they hit the ground they drove the entire city of Baghdad familiarizing themselves with every section. They mounted a video camera on the front vehicle and watched the tape at night, looking for possible threats and anything they should keep an eye out for.

According to the soldiers of

Shadow Force, that training was necessary, because everything that could happen to a patrol in Baghdad happened to them. They were sniped at, RPGs were shot at their convoy, an IED exploded just before their convoy reached it and received machinegun fire.

This unit conducted more convoy patrol missions and logged more miles in Baghdad than most regular troop units, such as infantry or cavalry companies did during the same time.

What made the Shadow Force so exemplary was how they all came together as one cohesive unit and the level of teamwork they achieved in such a short period of time.

Active duty and reservist soldiers voluntarily came together for one purpose, one goal and as one team to serve in a very dangerous capacity, in a very dangerous part of the world and at a very dangerous time. Together, they represented what the First Team motto of the prolific 1st Cavalry Division of Task Force Baghdad was really all about.

I was invited to go along with the Shadow Force

Left Above: SPC Fields served with the detachment from the beginning, Left Below: CPT Enneser and SSG Gray prepare for the day's mission, Below center: SSG Mosqueda was one of the mainstays of the Shadow Force from the beginning as well as SSG Garcia below.

The Um-Altalbul Mosque along the Airport Highway near the center of Baghdad was built for wealthy Sunni Muslims and became the source of many anti-US and anti-coalition announcements from the loudspeakers and was often used by insurgents to fight from. The convoy stopped because a roadside bomb was found. A Bradley Fighting Vehicle was dispatched to the location to add security.

and take pictures as often as I could. When OIF II kicked off, the PSD's three Humvees were open with no doors or armament of any kind. During this time I would ride behind the passenger seat taking pictures out the side of the moving vehicle.

Often we were caught in the more congested areas of downtown Baghdad where pedestrians were so close to the side of the road that it was impossible to have a weapon or a camera sticking out of the vehicle because someone could not only easily grab it and jerk it out of your hands, but you would be smacking people on the sides of their faces as the vehicle passed by.

When the detachment finally received up armor kits after the hottest action of the uprisings were over

in mid-July, I rode up by the machinegunner in the back of the pick-up style Humvee, so I could take pictures as the convoy moved at high speeds all over Baghdad. This worked out even better than before.

On several occasions LTC Welch would take me with him into the buildings to meet with people. It was my accepted responsibility to serve as the colonel's gopher boy, secretary and if the situation necessitated, body guard and bullet stopper as well. I am glad to say that no meeting ever went bad. I would like to think that I would react appropriately if it became necessary, but I don't know, and thank God I don't know... yet.

On one occasion I went with the colonel into a meeting (see June 13th e-mail), when we convoyed to a Karq

neighborhood of Baghdad where there had been a lot of action at the time. The Division Chaplain, LTC Moran was with us. I had been riding with SSG Gray in the lead vehicle and he was pretty nervous because the neighborhood was hot.

The locals were scurrying around as we pulled into the narrow alleys around the high-rise buildings, because they were afraid that the convoy would get hit with RPGs and they might get caught in the crossfire.

As I was getting out, Colonel Welch yelled at me to take my gear off and leave my weapon, pointing to himself, he said that this was the uniform. Without so much as a pocket knife the three officers, LTC Welch, Chaplain Moran and I walked rapidly into a dark building. We were met by the influential

businessman's personal security force. The three of us were enveloped by Iraqis toting small machineguns. We walked rapidly and nervously into the dark building that was without power. I was scared to death as we were led up two or three flights of stairs. I remembered resting in the fact that we had the Division Chaplain with us, thinking that surely that man was full of faith right now. After the meeting, I told the two higher ranking officers about how scared the situation made me, only to hear the chaplain tell us that he had been equally as scared.

I was only able to attend a handful of these meetings, but they were the most interesting and intense experiences of the entire tour.

It was because of the soldiers of Shadow Force and LTC Welch, that the world of Baghdad was opened up to me to photograph. I was able to experience some of the most interesting and intense situations of the whole tour of duty. I will be forever grateful to them for these memorable experiences.

February 25, 2004

Dear Family and Friends

Well I made it. I am in Kuwait and out in the middle of the desert. The desert here is so big and flat that there is not even a gopher mound to obstruct the view. There is a perfect curved horizon in all directions so that you could take an accurate sextant reading in all directions on dry land. The weather here is cold, dry and windy.

The travel over was well over thirty hours total with about 19 continuous hours on the same plane. The tent conditions are rough here because of the over-crowding with all the forces coming and going. There are lines for everything: food, bathroom, showers, Internet and coffee. The food here is good and I am happy to be here, but I am looking forward to moving north to Baghdad, which should be in two weeks.

So far we are getting along

E-MAILS FROM BAGHDAD

IN CHRONOLOGICAL ORDER

Kuwaiti Desert at Sunset. The landscape was so flat that a perfectly curved horizon formed in all directions.

as well as can be expected. I will try and get a photo for the next time I e-mail. Thank you for all the prayers,

Captain Tim Tate

February 27, 2004

There is a lot of running around here with the massive movement of troops. There is also a lot of camaraderie among the guardsmen.

So far nothing exciting except a bad case of food poisoning. I was unfortunate enough to eat that salis-bury steak also, but that's OK because I'm regular again thank you very much. Actually it was no laughing matter as a sergeant in my unit had to go to the medical facility and they ended up sticking a couple of IVs in him and pounded him with medication. I had a really easy time in comparison with his ordeal.

The group of soldiers I work with are simply the some of the best soldiers I have ever been associated with and we are all getting along under some rather adverse conditions. We all stay in the same tent together with no separation from male and female, officer and enlisted. I told the females last night that contrary to popular belief that they are not all sugar and spice.

I am doing well and look forward to hearing from you.

Soldiers entered Iraq after spending two to four weeks in the middle of the Kuwaiti desert living in tents like this one.

February 28, 2004

This will be the last one for awhile. You may be won-dering why I am e-mailing so much. My pay was all messed up and so I have had to log on every so many hours to try and get it fixed. I am happy to say that the pay problem is now fixed. It is a major effort to get onto a computer around here with many long lines. Each line is typically greater than two hours. When I am on the Internet I try to get the most out of it and send off a little blurb to all of you. No I am not homesick, although I miss everyone very much.

I did my laundry in a sink for the first time this morning.

March 12, 2004

From Baghdad with Love

After two months and one week of call up, train up, ramp up, and prep up, we finally reached Baghdad. The convoy up from Kuwait itself was quite eventful with two vehicles breaking down and the highway was closed because Improvised Explo-sive Devices (IED) "bombs" were found and had to be detonated in place. The army has gotten the art of finding these bombs and detonating them without hurting anyone down really well. It was a typical military operation as 12 hours of driving were crammed into three days.

It looks like I will be work-ing the night shift for the 1st CAV Division. This will be a boring uneventful job that will not allow me to do any traveling. I will try and get outside the wire as much as possible and see things and hopefully report on them,

CPT Tate in Kuwait standing at the corner of SNAFU BLVD and BOHICA DR. These WWII acronyms stand for Situation Normal, All @##$ Up and Bend Over Here It Comes Again.

but as of right now I have a very safe and boring job inside a large building working behind a computer and telephone.

If you would like to send something small that's OK but please don't go to crazy as I have too carry everything with me from the Post Office on foot after it gets inspected. Please don't send any chocolate as it's up in the eighties here in the latter part of winter of Baghdad.

March 20, 2004

I am still not acclimated to the night hours while trying to sleep during the day. For whatever reason I am not able to adjust readily and my sleep pattern is suffering greatly. I'm pretty miserable right now.

One of the first nights that I worked, a bomb at the Mt Lebanon Hotel exploded and I spent the first four hours just tracking all the information about the casualties

for the major. It's amazing what hits the news and what doesn't. There was another major incident that morning and so far the news station hasn't picked up on it.

Today I had the opportunity to fly in a Blackhawk helicopter for the first time. It was an amazing experience as you can see by one of the photos. Blackhawks can pull a lot more G forces than the old Huey helicopters from the Vietnam era.

The chopper flew nap of the earth, about 40 feet off the ground, pulling up for trees and power lines and then after the bird would clear the lines, they would reverse the pitch of the main rotor blades diving the chopper back down.

Everywhere we flew, the children would run out and wave at us. It's amazing how we have been received the entire time here. I am convinced that the Iraqis are very grateful and glad to have us here until the job is done.

The neighborhoods ranged from absolutely filthy slums to some incredibly beautiful villas that appeared to be built in a fortified manner similar to that what Ude and Kuse were found hiding in. God bless and please e-mail a letter and let me know what's going on in the states.

_____

March 29, 2004

I have nightly access to the Internet and some time to put these e-mails together. Last night's shift was hellish. After being on the M-16 qualification range out in the sunlight all day, I was exhausted when I started the

night shift. I did alright until 0430 rolled around (4:30 AM). I crashed and became what is commonly referred to as combat ineffective. I was toast. All I could do was persevere. Today I slept for almost nine hours, and I'm a completely different person. It is now 0030 hours (30 minutes past midnight) and I'm just as awake as can be.

GOOD NEWS ON THE FRONT: Tonight we caught 14 people in an IED bomb factory, another 6 in a weapons storage house, and another sought after fugitive turned himself in. The good news is local polls show that most Iraqi's, to include the Shiites, do not want an Islamic theocracy like Iran.

THE BAD NEWS: The media is releasing articles spelling doom and gloom for the acceptance of the interim governing counsel and the interim constitution. There is a lot of talk about Ayatollah Sistani creating a very well organized anti-constitution and anti-government lobbying effort from within his religious sphere of influence.

OPED: It appears to me that the US has created it's own adversary by condescending to this Ayatollah Sistani by giving him more credibility than he ever had

Shia Muslims watching their flocks was a common scene that many soldiers saw on their convoy north out of Kuwait. Most of these Shia Muslims welcomed soldiers and convoys with smiles and waves. Many requested food and water by motioning with their hands.

This is just one small section of the enormous graveyard of military vehicles such as tanks and artillery pieces left behind by the retreating Iraqi Army after the United States invaded Kuwait. The only way for Hussein's army to retreat was along the highway between Baghdad and Kuwait which put all the vehicles inline. This made it very easy for American helicopters and attack planes such as the A-10 Warthog to destroy them. The final battlefield in the war was commonly referred to as the Highway of Death.

or would have had on his own. His credibility and name recognition have been greatly elevated by the US military and media. The more resistance he can make with the help of all the US government and media attention, the more leverage he can have for his demands and for his cooperation.

I talked with a military police officer and an interpreter

The tent at the Baghdad International Airport (BIAP) had a piece of shrapnel from a Russian mortar land on top of the canvas burning a hole through the matierial.

An old Iraqi Army tank fighting position. The tank would park in the large hole behind the berm keeping its silhouette to a minimum and also keeping its tracks and drive train below ground. This fighting position was probably part of the defensive preparation for the recent US led invasion. Note the individual fighting positions or fox holes around the tank hole.

for the new Iraqi police liaison we have here about the Iraqi police. They both agreed that the Iraqi police are doing well.

He also said the government is nervous about the June 30th Transition of Authority. The Facility Protection Service (FPS) or glorified security guards are causing a lot of trouble and the source of a lot of corruption in Baghdad.

The soldiers are streaming into Baghdad from Kuwait as we enter into the heaviest part of the change of forces, the largest in the history of military operations I'm told. I describe this whole operation as a "very well

organized mass confusion". I mean this in a complimentary sort of way. There are a lot difficulties as most of the details for this operation were never thought through well enough. However, the individual soldiers and lower level units are all working together to make the handover of authority take place. I have been very impressed with the teamwork that I have seen. Absolutely amazed is more realistic.

April 02, 2004

Today I moved two miles north of here to Camp

Victory North where I am supposed to live for the next year. It's near the Palaces by the lake that I sent pictures of last time I e-mailed you all. I have my own air conditioned room now.

It is the smallest room I've ever had to live in but it's more than I've ever had from the army before. This is much better than sleeping in the dirt in southern California's Death Valley as I have often had to do.

The temperature has been up in the eighties and nineties and will soon be over a hundred degrees daily.

Take note of the pictures I sent. The National Guard picture's silhouette: truth hurts. The tanks that can barely be seen are Iraqi tanks. We killed them all along the "Highway of Death" when they were trying to flee north from Kuwait in 1991.

There was only one major highway for them to drive along and this put them all in a line which made it incredibly easy for helicopters and planes to swoop down on them and kill many at a time.

Despite all the bad news on the networks, I assert that most Iraqis are glad we're here and don't want us to leave quite yet. It is a difficult, dangerous, and very

National Guard soldiers set this sign up as a joke. Many of us National Guard soldiers resembled this remark.

3

exciting time to be here. This coming year will have an enormous impact on the rest of the world for a very long time.

I feel, as many do, that this is a huge contribution that I am making not only to the American and the Iraqi people, but also for the entire world. It is crucial that we finish the job and get it done right.

THE GOOD NEWS: More and more schools are opening up and soldiers have begun delivering backpacks to young students at these schools. The backpacks are purchased in the states and filled with pencils, paper and stuff, then citizens send them over here and the soldiers deliver them.

This is a big plus in winning the hearts and minds of the future Iraqi voters. More hospital modernizations are taking place to include training of doctors and nurses by military medical personnel. These Iraqi medical personnel did not receive the best education possible under the old regime.

The biggest and most expensive of all Civil Affairs work projects is the sewer infrastructure in my opinion. The massive undertaking of rebuilding or building of the sewage treatment infrastructure will probably never be as popular as it should. It will have the biggest impact on health and welfare of the people of Iraq where millions live in their own filth. The military is directly and indirectly involved in bringing online refurbished and new sewage treatment plants all over Iraq, but particularly in and around the Baghdad area. I can't give any numbers or cost projection but eliminating the green smelly ponded water in many of the Baghdad neighborhoods is costly and will probably be

Soldiers began sending letters home asking for their fishing gear to be sent out to them so they could enjoy their time off. Fish over 36 inches long could be caught regularly. Note the weapon on the back of the angler.

the least reported or the least remembered improvements left behind by the occupation (Liberation) forces.

Most nations with militaries in this Iraqi theater have chosen to stay the course along with President Bush and we need to be glad about these allies versus spending too much time lamenting over those who have chosen to reconsider their involvement with this Operation

Iraqi Freedom.

THE BAD NEWS: Even though the anti-coalition forces are few, it only takes a success once every two weeks to put a big damper on things. The car bombing of Al Hyat Hotel on March 17th was the last really big ugly event until the 9 dead Americans yesterday on the 1st of April. In that time span we have arrested about 100 bad guys to include

enough rocket and mortar launching insurgents to put a significant dent in the nightly attacks. Tonight we don't have any reports of detaining insurgents noted yet. That was not the case on most nights this past month.

The different factions, some religious, some political, and some power hungry, are taking advantage of this unstable time to gain power and control over the local populace and build their numbers.

This includes Shiite clerics who muster their own army of up to 10,000 untrained militants for the Ayatollah Sistani. They are all targeting the youth in universities where militant fraternities are harassing other students and inflicting fear on professors.

The positive is that the Iraqi military and police force is recruiting thousands, to the hundreds of recruits of the would be power mongers. The new Iraqi defense forces and police now number in the many tens of thousands and are being trained by US trainers. They have a

The hulk of a Russian T-55 tank now silent still guarding Baghdad's southern entrance.

The Transition of Authority ceremony between 1st Cavalry Division and 1st Armor Division took place downtown in the Green Zone under the Cross Swords where Hussein held his military parades. Major General Chiarelli is in the middle and can be distinguished by his brown suede cavalry boots. To the left of him is Major General Dempsey of the 1st Armored Division Iron Soldiers with his staff. To the right of General Chiarelli is his own staff.

the money coming in and flowing down to the normal citizen and make sure they know where it is coming from. 3. Bolster a strong professional police force. 4. Limit the influence of the different factions on young people by heavily patrolling university campuses and arresting young recruits who are engaged in aggressive bullying and violent activity and then kick them out of the university. Don't allow these young people who have been swayed to get an education. They're going to have to beef up campus security a lot more. 5. Get the real elections going and do whatever it takes to make sure the voting is fair and complete and that people can vote without threat. The normal population does not want an Islamic state or a divided Iraq and they will vote as such. 6. Continue to win the hearts and minds of the young and impressionable with efforts such as backpacks. 7. Stay the course. If we give up now because of an election and withdraw troops, it will be much worse in the future than it was under Hussein.

long way to go and there is a lot of uncertainty, but the numbers are being stacked heavily in favor of the forthcoming Iraqi government.

Japan, who has sent a medical type Brigade to southern Iraq is being swindled out of millions by local sheiks. They waited for the Japanese to set up base camp for the 500 soldiers out in the open desert of completely useless ground that won't support agriculture of any kind and then demanded $800 an acre per year. Right now the

negotiations are between 60 and 80 dollars an acre per year. The Japanese are having a hard time dealing with this type of negotiation where they have to pay an outrageous sum of money to be able to come in here and

help make life better for the Iraqi people.

OPED: The keys for democracy to be successful in Iraq are: 1. Get the economy going and the young men gainfully employed. 2. Get the oil flowing and

April 06, 2004

Moqtada al-Sadr, the Islamic cleric who is described as an Islamic extremist, has built up a following of Islamic fundamentalists all over Iraq by drawing mainly from impoverished discontented

A Blackhawk takes off during the Transition of Authority on April 9th 2004. Right Place, Right Time.

The parade grounds with the crossed swords had many beautifully landscaped and architectural features such as this large water fountain pond with lighting towers dotting the skies.

Luckily for us the man and his key lieutenants aren't that bright. He decided to come out of his pacifistic non-hostile stand and go on the offensive during the transition of authority. This means that Mehdi militia, as they're called, are taking on twice as many American soldiers all over Iraq with two and a half as many soldiers in the Baghdad area. If the young cleric had waited two more weeks he would have less than half the number of US soldiers to face. Information about the changing out of troops and the numbers involved have been all over the news media for some time. Evidently the militants don't know how to read and don't watch Fox News.

Their fighting skills aren't

battle needless to say, and last night it was like a shooting gallery at the county fair out there for our soldiers.

Tonight, it's a lot more quiet out there and the three-star general, or at least his office has officially declared that the Mehdi militia is hostile and are to be engaged and destroyed on sight. Sucks to be them.

THE BAD NEWS: The Mehdi militia did carry out one ambush on two cargo trucks that did not have any armor. They have been able to kill and injure only a few of our soldiers, but a few is too many.

They were successfully able to coerce or collaborate with Iraqi police and the new Iraqi Army and they took over police stations that were

Muslim communities in the slums of Iraq. Since the fall of the old regime, he has recruited and organized a militia of poorly trained followers. He has initiated hostile attacks against mostly Iraqi police stations and other government buildings, and carried out coordinated attacks and ambushes on coalition forces in several cities and has now publicly threatened for a long drawn out violent front against coalition forces.

THE GOOD NEWS: This Islamic extremist with a strong following of about ten thousand untrained, but heavily armed young men, has finally showed his true colors and we can now go after him and his followers.

The US forces would not touch him before in an effort to win the hearts and minds and the trust of the local populace in our commitment to freedom and the right to protest and due process. We were monitoring the situation knowing full well that he intended on taking over

These viewing stands were built for Saddam Hussein's military parade field. American soldiers can be seen preparing for the ceremony in front of the stands.

someday, but we thought he was smart enough not to begin hostile activities until we were gone and he stood a much better chance of carrying out a bloody coup just like Saddam Hussein did 25 years ago.

any better than their plani-skills. Members of Mehdi militia are attacking US M1 Abrams tanks and M2 Brad-lys in front of police stations with rifles (AK-47s) and Rocket Propelled Grenades (RPGs). They're losing this

abandoned. This made for only a few fatalities. These facilities were easily retaken over by US forces or Iraqi police. There were many desertions of Iraqi soldiers that have just completed basic training. There is a lot of discouragement among the leadership here because the Iraqi defense forces did not perform up to the level that US commanders had hoped.

OPED: I have stated before that one of the key tenets for a successful democratic Iraq is to have a highly professional police force. After just one year, they still have a long way to go.

I have met some soldiers with credible experience that say many of the police officers are top notch and others that claim they're a bunch of rogues that can't be counted on. We have certainly seen evidence that both of these opinions are correct. However, with just one year of experience and

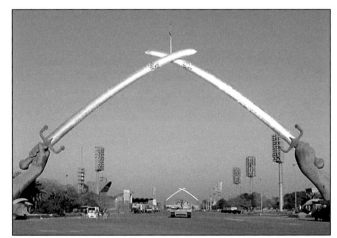

having been brought up under the harsh whip of fear, it is easy to look through the average inexperienced police officers' eyes. It is easy to see that fear and lack of confidence in their units prevails over their desire to help Iraq successfully reach a free democratic sovereign state.

There are many stories coming out of people coming out of their homes in the morning and being approached by groups of men with weapons. They are told to stop going to work or their wife and kids will be murdered or other

similar threats. The militants obviously know who they are, what they do, and where

they live.

The US Army is unable to protect these people and their families 24 hours a day,

but we are expecting them to be the soldiers we need them to be.

Above: 1st Cavalry Division Honor Guard normally are mounted on horses, but this time they were on foot in downtown Baghdad. Right: covered walkway at the parade grounds, Left: M1 Abrams Main Battle Tank under crossed swords. Below: Both honor guards from both divisions participated as General Dempsey and his Command Sergeant Major uncase the colors during the ceremony.

My optimistic outlook is that in another year we will make enormous progress towards a large police force

that continuously weeds its ranks of the weak and corrupt. One year is simply not enough time to build and instill the confidence and trust of fellow police officers in a brand new police force that is being birthed on the battlefield of Baghdad. Three years is even more realistic. We must finish the job right or all that has transpired will be for naught.

April 16, 2004

This is not intended to be a form of whining on my part but rather just letting you all know the joys and the pains of working in Baghdad, Iraq on the night shift. I have much to be grateful for as

you probably have seen by now. I have seen some amazing things and I live in a relatively clean and somewhat safe environment compared to my life in the combat arms such as infantry and combat engineers. This deployment is an absolute dream compared to most of the major training events I have been a part of.

There are some problems to working at the Division command center at night. My body so far has not, and will not adjust to the sleep cycle. I am absolutely loopy at night when I am supposed to be getting things done and then as the sun comes up my body decides it's no longer tired and wakes up.

I can usually count on two to three hours of sleep during the day and laying in bed for many more hours hoping for just one more hour of sleep. This will go for about very little interaction. All the socializing I have done the six months before deployment has no doubt made it more difficult being the odd-man-out around here.

There is no opportunity to go to church for me and maybe I need to start looking at finding a new assignment. I hope that this did not sound like a snivel session.

Today's OPED: I'd like to compare Christian martyrdom to the Islamic martyrdom. I have not researched this topic at all and all my opinions are purely based on stereotypes that I have picked up on through talking to several Iraqis here. The local cleric Moqtada al-Sadr has called for a Jihad, which the local Iraqis claim he has

Above: A typical neighborhood in southern Baghdad taken from a Blackhawk helicopter. Below: A typical hand powered Ferris wheel in Baghdad.

three days until I reach the point that I sleep for seven to nine hours to make up for the previous deprivation. Then I will have a couple of days of survivable sleep of about four to six hours a day and then the cycle starts over, or so it seems.

Surprisingly a big problem that I am facing is the loneliness from being separated out from the unit that I came here with. As I am coming off shift there might be one hour of overlap and maybe I can see them and talk to them but more often than not, that isn't possible.

There is a positive to this, and that is a lot of the people I came here with are not exactly behaving like soldiers ought to behave and maybe it's for the best that there is from my previous experiences with army chapels, there is little desire for me to go either. I am no longer able to enjoy the source of fellowship that I had found within the group I came with, and this too is taking a toll.

The night shift crew seems to take care of each other much better and the battle heats up at night making the monitoring of the Baghdad a lot more interesting. I have access to the Internet for many hours during the job.

There are some opportunities for me during the day when I am off that the day shift doesn't have, as an example the ceremony I just attended. I was able to get in on that at the last minute because I wasn't working during the day. Well I think

A similar neighborhood as previous page. Note the ponding of water as it had rained the previous three days. Both the regional geology and the unmaintained sewer system prevented groundwater from draining. The large ponds simply baked dry in the sun. Many of the ponds that formed when it rained, became instant cesspools.

no right to do. I have seen the reports coming in of these people assaulting tanks on foot with AK-47s and dying, proving that they are obeying him dutifully.

These Muslims, mostly from the slums of eastern Baghdad as I have stated before, are consciously deciding to become martyrs. At first glance there really is a tight symbiotic relationship between martyrs and American soldiers here. The Arab wants to die for Moqtada al-Sadr and the soldier helps him meet his goal; no problem.

I really feel that these people have been victimized again by having been born into the wrong location and social disposition as to be naturally drawn into the control of yet one more lunatic.

This cleric who has called for Jihad has taken advan-

tage of the ignorant people who are looking to anyone who can provide strong leadership and something that they can hang onto in an unstable and scary time. This Moqtada al-Sadr has taken advantage of the lost scared sheep and has recruited them so he can lead them to the slaughter to his own glory.

I found it interesting that the Islamic Jihad requires that the would-be martyrs go out shooting in a blaze of glory. On the contrary, Christian martyrs that I have read about did not choose their fate but either by providence or by chance in a "free will" world found themselves in the horrible situation where they either denied Christ or lost their life.

They were often tested for their faith and many times they were falsely accused, but in my mind Christian

martyrs never defended themselves against their accusers. This is very much the contrast with going down with blazing AK-47s.

I found it interesting to note these differences keeping in mind that the violent aggressive and premeditated Islamic martyr, though it

seems obviously wrong to those raised in the Christian culture, probably looks intuitively correct to the Muslim. Choosing to go "postal for paradise", which in this case is really choosing to die for the desires of Moqtada al-Sadr. This aggressive martyrdom probably looks

A typical palm tree grove from the Blackhawk. Many fire fights took place from groves just like this one.

much more heroic not only in the eyes of young Muslim men, but also in the eyes of the world. I can earnestly see how the Christian form of martyrdom looks odd to the world.

In Christianity martyrdom is not chosen by the martyr. The martyr did nothing to earn this title or award if you will. How can somebody who happens to have their life taken from them be up for some sort of super status in heaven over someone who may have actually been much better at practicing their religion but was smart enough to avoid the bad neighborhoods in this world?

Several questions arise then about the rules of martyrdom for Christianity. If you are not given any choices but just assassinated are you still a martyr as compared to someone who was repeatedly

A typical neighborhood in northern Baghdad. The view is actually from Saddam Hussein's private hospital on the north side of the Tigris River.

tortured for their faith in attempt to get them to deny the faith?

If God has called you to be a soldier and it's his will that you fight and die on the battlefield, because you were obedient to Christ, can you be considered a martyr?

Don't worry about me. I am not declaring any Jihads. Please keep us all in your prayers.

April 21, 2004

Submission/Obedience, and Decapitating Reservist Leadership

The last e-mail went out prematurely. I had started preparing it when I had to jump and run to take care of a report. My immediate higher ranking boss sat down at the computer and evidently hit the send button just to get rid of my work. I'm not happy about that, but what do you say to higher ranking officer in the army? "Yes sir! Thank you very much sir! May I have another?" This brings up the question what do you do when the worldly boss you have to submit to is somebody you have a really hard time looking up to in any way or form?

I have been conviced on this point of submission and obedience from the reli-

Above: The Washington State University Flag with all the Football, Girl's Soccer and Volley Ball Players signatures along with the coaches and town mayor who is also the main announcer at sporting events. My good friend Keith Bloom, who works in construction management at WSU, serves as city council-man and also is owner and proprietor along with his wife Jan of Cafe Moro coffee shop in downtown Pullman, gathered the signatures on a cougar flag and sent it to me. This flag was used to inspire many Coug fans serving in Baghdad. Now that is a buddy for you.

Sunrise over Z Lake. The lake, like many others in southwestern Baghdad, was dug out along with an intricate canal system to drain the swamp lands that were unusable. The land was cleared for the airport and many palaces. This lake was part of the private hunting and fishing grounds for Ude and Kuse and is stocked with popular sport-fish from around the world.

gious influence in my life. Remembering that many of the people on my e-mail list aren't exactly the most churched or religious people I would like to share some thoughts on military submission and obedience.

Submit and Obey are dirty words in any society. These are not the words that people like to talk about. I have never heard anyone brag about how they submitted to a jerk of a boss who shouldn't be in charge of a pencil let alone a person. Instead I have heard all my life people bragging about how they told their boss to go and !#@$#$.

Submitting and obeying in the military should be the key cornerstone for all military operations and for all militaries around the world. One person gets told to go do something and then he or she goes and does it. That however, is not what any

The bridge that connected North Victory (Now Camp Liberty) with South Victory (Now Camp Victory) where the Water Palace is located.

military considers it's cornerstone. All the doctrine in the US Army is written from the perspective of the sender, or the order giver and not the

doer, or the order receiver. All doctrine that I have ever seen is written from the leadership perspective as "this is how you order subordinates to do a mission and then this is how you make sure they do it." How interesting that we don't think about writing, "This is how you receive an order and this is how you carry it out."

How does this affect the military? It can make for a lot of yelling and screaming because there is an inherent need to maintain control over subordinates who are also being trained for bold aggressive leadership and not for submitting and obeying. The army loves to develop strong bold aggressive leadership in soldiers at

11

A typical busy commercial street in western Baghdad.

Above: Commonly found landmines and grenades in Iraq. Below: A Rocket Propelled Grenade (RPG) Launcher. The actual grenade is the cone shaped black warhead at the left end of the launcher. This was one of the more effective weapons from the old Soviet military and was used extensively by insurgents during the Medhi Militia (Sadr City) and Falluja uprisings during OIF II.

all levels and those character traits that are the opposite of leadership, submitting and obedience, are some sort of extraneous attribute that some people have to learn along the way by accident. It is always interesting to note how leadership demands total submission but boldly stands up for their command in such a way that your high-

I have seen and heard much less of it in more recent times. There has been a large improvement in the military with regard to the yelling, screaming and confrontations among leadership and I am more than impressed by the US Army, both from the success rate over the past 15 years and from the internal improvements I have

poorly defined work relationships lobby and vie for top dog position. We are all supposed to work together to take care of the commanding general.

While working the night shift I had to ask the colonel about answering a request for information from our counterparts at the next higher echelon, the guys that

A typical Shia farm south of Baghdad. After the photograph was taken the family rushed out to wave at the helicopter.

er commanders don't want to mess with you or tell you what to do.

You see it from time to time, but I must confess that

witnessed myself over the last 18 years.

On this deployment I have run into this problem where soldiers and officers in

work for the three-star General Sanchez. He rebuffed me harshly for even asking him that question because "He didn't have to answer

to them because he worked directly for a two-star general. The major that I was on the phone with asking me for information was not somebody he had to answer to. "Colonels!" I didn't tell him to wake up and smell the coffee because the man I was talking to on the phone worked directly for the three-star general for whom his two-star general worked directly for. I just let it go and decided to stand back and let the matter settle out.

In the past week my colonel has become more amicable and is doing a better job of playing well with others, but the problems that we are facing with some verbal abuse from these active duty guys to some of our National Guard soldiers is more difficult to swallow knowing that the colonel doesn't

the active duty soldiers who are supposed to be getting at least 90-140 days of training a year. Certain jobs are more suited for the reservists such as truck driving and communications. Once you learn how to operate a big truck for example, you only need 20 days of practice a year to maintain your skills. For most job skills such as infantry, mechanic or medical field occupations, you simply can't maintain your skills.

This is particularly true for leadership skills. Mid level leadership of battalion and brigade units where majors, lieutenant colonels and

A family comes out of their home in southern Baghdad to wave at the US Military convoy as it passes by.

Discipline and prompt obedience to orders is what the US Army is all about. Could not resist this one.

answer to authority very well himself. One of them hinted to me that there may be some restructuring going on next month if matters don't improve.

THE DILEMMA OF CALLING UP RESERVISTS TO WORK FOR ACTIVE DUTY OFFICERS: The reservist components are there to be called up to fill and fulfill the active duty army's needs. It is inherently obvious that a military unit that can only train, at best 20-40 days a year, is going to have some skill and competency issues as compared to

colonels have 12-25 years of active duty experience to develop their leadership skills and to become brainwashed into the military way of life.

Higher levels of leadership such as division and corps with two and three-star generals in charge and colonels and one-stars running around taking care of things have 20-30 years of experience to develop their leadership and their bearing.

When the reserve unit gets called up, the leadership has to start working directly under and meld in with all the other unit leadership and

they have to do this as if they have been on active duty the whole time and there aren't any real differences. Obviously there is a problem with them working directly under and melding in as if there weren't any differences.

ACTIVE DUTY JERKS: One of the things I soon learned about being a reserve officer is, when you get called up you often get screwed over by those active duty jerks. Everyone told me as I was preparing for this deployment "Don't

bother preparing for your job, because you know as soon as you get there, they're going to just pull you out of your unit and make you the assistant to the head gopher boy for the general's staff." It was always discouraging but I came here prepared for that.

I should give you an excellent example of getting screwed over by active duty so you know exactly what I'm talking about. On the way up from Kuwait my convoy pulled into one of the

Children surrounding the convoy while we stopped.

13

major stops along the way. I went into the movement control team's building. All the soldiers on duty were officers. They were all national guard officers who had been taken away from their units and put out in the middle of Iraq at this military truck stop called Scania and they were all doing jobs that should have been done by sergeants.

I talked to one of them who told me his plight. He had taken over as company commander for a transportation unit in the deep south somewhere two years before being activated, and had been very active in recruiting soldiers and building up his unit's size in the number of soldiers and its overall strength.

He was actually ready to be transferred out, but insisted on staying with the unit as they deployed to Iraq. When he got to Kuwait they took him away from his unit and ordered him to go to this truck stop about three hundred miles away from where his unit eventually was stationed. His job became the night shift watch to check convoys in as they come and go at night.

His unit carried out their jobs that they were supposed do, i.e. the jobs that they had enlisted for, mostly truck drivers, without him. This captain was getting his proficiency rating for being a commander in combat in theater, while he was pulling a sergeant or staff sergeant's job as a night shift desk clerk, three hundred miles away from the unit he was supposed to be commanding. The salt in the open wound was that the active duty decision maker, probably some lieutenant colonel took all of his soldiers and put an active duty lieutenant in charge of them. He was one miserable

Summer light reflects off of one of the many palm trees that lined the lake where the Al Fah Water Palace was located.

man and I don't blame him for his bitterness.

The old timers in the Guard used to tell me how the

active duty would take all the vehicles away from the Guardsmen and give them to active duty soldiers who didn't care about their use and abuse. This was because the National Guard trains less and puts less miles and hours on their equipment which is very important for trucks and earth moving equipment. This does not

happen as much any more or at all from what I can see.

THOSE NASTY GUARDSMAN: 20-30 pounds overweight, sloppy posture with little or no military bearing, doesn't know how to write a report or memorandum to military standard, first name basis or blood relation to many subordinate soldiers and

Above and Below: The Market street in the Green Zone in downtown Baghdad where local merchants are allowed to sell their merchandise to soldiers. Pirated DVDs of movies that had just opened in the theaters in the US could be purchased for as little as $3.00 on this street.

carrying the latest and greatest equipment. Many states purchased the latest greatest equipment for their soldiers as a guilt offering. Most active duty soldiers have only seen pictures of some of this equipment. This is what I

with being activated away from career and family, something that reservists are not accustomed to.

The active duty needs the manpower of the reserve units to accomplish their missions successfully. Their

crucial both for the active duty officer and for the reserve soldiers at the ground level.

There is a legitimate problem with reserve leaders showing up to go to battle with some legitimate defi-

reality. I think with regard to the higher ranking active duty officers, they tend to believe that the problems with reserve leadership is larger than it really is. Many of these older active duty officers being of middle age

imagine to be the first impression that many reservists officers make when they first show up to their new place of duty.

The active duty army's high ranking officers have to try and communicate with entire battalion and brigade leadership staffs that don't know how to use the latest FM radios, don't know how to write orders or give them to their subordinates, and are showing up on the battlefield often with serious interpersonal problems associated

The Al Fah Water Palace was an architectural masterpiece for photographers and a maintenance nightmare for engineers. The above and below pictures are of the same main entrance from opposite directions.

careers are often dependant on how well the reserve soldiers do their jobs on the battlefield and therefore the proper leadership of those soldiers on the battlefield is

ciencies in their leadership skills and inabilities to work and meld in with the active duty counterparts.

However, this problem is more perception than

and hard headed, having grown naturally accustomed to things being exactly their way to include how soldiers look and act, being quite intolerant of reservists.

The problem with legitimate leadership deficiencies is difficult to do anything about. The inexperience of reserve officers and the inability to interface within active duty commands smoothly and quickly will always be a problem.

On the other side of the

Above: Right: The main room of the Water Palace shows the magnificent architecture but was also poorly constructed. Most of Hussein's many elaborate palaces had one main grand room that was highlighted by a high domed ceiling. Below and below right: The furniture that had somehow survived the looting after the invasion was usually in the French Louis the XIV style and very cheaply constructed. One should always sit carefully on any of the former regime furniture or else one might fall through and get stuck.

coin is the perception and intolerance from some high ranking officers towards reservists, particularly those from the National Guard. This negative view towards reservists can be the driving force behind the decapitation of the head leadership, but more often than not, results in communication barriers which always affects the soldiers below.

There is a real problem when large numbers of soldiers on the battlefield aren't being used effectively because of leadership issues. It has been publicly reported for a long time that the Task Force Baghdad which is the 1st Cavalry Division is composed of 40% reservists. That means out of the 30 plus thousand soldiers here, approximately 13,000 are reservists many of whom are part of the combat fighting force. Not being able to use this large number of soldiers effectively could be a very serious problem.

April 21, 2004

One person has already e-mailed in asking if I intended to say that the 13,000 National Guardsmen are poorly managed and misled and therefore not a part of the battle and are just deadweight at this point. That is not at all what I intended to say. I was writing from a hypothetical situation where if the situation exists, then there is a problem and historically yes it has been a

The Al Fah Palace, or the Water Palace as the soldiers called it, was one of Hussein's greatest palaces. This enormous building along with many others were built on islands in the middle of lakes. The lakes were manmade when Hussein ordered the swamp lands to the southwest of Baghdad be drained for the building of the modern day airport. These three pictures depict the grand entrance. The left two pictures are from inside the building.

problem here and there. The initial reports on the reservist brigade are excellent.

THE ARMY'S SOLUTION: ARMY OF ONE! The army has been pushing the propaganda messages down for many years trying to sway various attitudes of all soldiers within it's ranks and the "Army of One" message is no different. There has always been a problem with the "Us-Them" mentality among units, rank echelons, active/reserve components and branches of service such as marines and army. This Us-Them mentality has always retarded cooperation and deterred the efficient carrying out of successful operations at all levels.

This "Army of One" concept has helped, but it is always up to the higher ranking chain of command as to how to implement the new policies. If the generals set the example of noncompliance, then I guarantee that anyone trying to do things correctly under them will be looked down on.

If the generals set the example of total acceptance and compliance then I guarantee that the subordinates

had better be on the bandwagon waving the policy flag. It is absolutely a direct reflection on the leadership at all levels as to whether the "Army of One" concept is implemented and we really are an army of one, and it is also a direct reflection of leadership at all levels if it is being ignored and it's back to the same ol' same ol'.

As I stated before, the previous leadership under LTG Sanchez did a lot of this decapitation of reservist leadership. That is not the case now I am happy to say. The 1st Cavalry Division, under Major General Chiarelli, made it plain to us that they were doing everything in their power to keep all the units intact and bring them up to speed with the active duty. God bless them for that but in several cases I believe they have taken this too far and are maintaining unit leadership integrity in place where they should invite individual reservists to go home, if only for the benefit of the reserve soldiers.

With that said I am grateful for the new policies of this new leadership taking over Task Force Baghdad and will gladly put up with some of the negative aspects from this. I am glad to be with my unit that I grew attached to during the train up at Ft.

ing from the military side of the house. You probably all think I have this sort of cushy life here in which all I do is travel around and take

going around. Evidently this is the rainy season. There has been high winds and thunder and lightening storms here these past cou-

because it's too dangerous for them. The lightening will set off most blasting caps because most of them are electrical.

Above two photographs: Two views from the balcony of the Water Palace. Above right: one of the many corridors in the upper floors of the Water Palace. Right: Author in the main room. Far right: The staircases were wonderfully done in Italian marble, but were constantly falling apart and in need of repair.

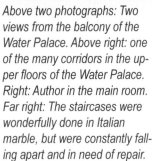

Lewis and I will tolerate this night shift, as it is my lot in life. I am striving to submit and obey.

April 25, 2004

I'm afraid I only have more pictures of palaces and noth-

pictures of palaces and then write lengthy e-mails. Oh if only that were the truth.

Everything here is fine except for a little bit of a cold

ple of days. It was interesting to note that during the thunder and lightening storms no terrorists were working. We believe it's

Some positive stories to help counterweight the gloom and doom. During the initial uprising of Moqtada al-Sadr in the Sadr Slums of eastern Baghdad, there were 8 CAV soldiers killed and tens wounded. Many of those soldiers who were wounded in the surprise attack actually were rescued by Iraqis from the slums who came out into the streets to pick up wounded GIs and help them to their units or in one case the Iraqi man put the wounded soldier in his car and drove him to a military hospital. That story didn't get told I bet.

One of the horror stories from the Hussein regime that I recently heard about came from a Kurdish man I know. He told me that back in the 70s after Hussein gassed the Kurds, the local orphanages were filled with surviving children. Hussein's military raided the orphanages and took off with all the 10 and 11 year old kids.

The girls were all raped by the soldiers and essentially were made into sex slaves. Some of them went into prostitution to make money for whomever, and some were made into gifts to high ranking Ba'ath party members. They all had the same mission. Be a sex toy for whomever and listen in on all the conversations and report anyone who is talking bad about Saddam Hussein. This plan worked well I am told and many of his adver-saries lost their heads.

The little boys were all gathered up and sent through a brainwashing military camp in which they were trained to believe that their souls belonged to Saddam Hussein. They somehow ended up in the Fedayin or the Republican Guard somewhere as faithful brain-washed soldiers who would die for Hussein. Keep in mind this was told to me by a Kurdish man.

One thing is becoming clear: the 1st Cavalry Division is turning up the heat to an all out boil on this Baghdad stew. The units from the 1st Cavalry are focusing on the worst neighbor-hoods. It was because of the presence of soldiers in the eastern Baghdad slums that things began to heat up. We're out there every day and night. It's be-coming obvi-ous that this is a whole new fight.

I am con-fident that we will win this fight just fine, but it's the fights at home and the internal corruption that seems to flourish so well that these are fights I don't think we can win.

On a hap-pier note. I finally was able to enter into one of the palaces and will enter into more soon. I have some pictures now and I will send some tomorrow.

This is the patio to one of the downtown palaces that was taken over by the US and made into a resort called Freedom's Rest where soldiers could go to get away from combat fatigue for three days.

19

A main palace in downtown Baghdad used by Saddam Hussein and his regime was severely damaged by the initial "shock and awe" attack which used large missiles and precision guided bombs dropped from Air Force planes.

April 26, 2004

Please keep in mind that I am very tired and groggy as I write this. Tonight's pictures are from one of the many palaces near the airport. It was the first time I was able to get into one of these palaces and it turned out to be quite a sight. I ran out of battery power and couldn't take anymore pictures, but I have received an invitation to come back.

I also have received another invitation to go and visit a major that I met coming up who works in the really big house that you saw pictures from yesterday. Can't wait. It's amazing how the only opportunity I have to do something here is to visit these palaces.

There is a war on outside the wire and people are dying out there just a few miles to the west while I play tourist. This is my lot in life and I will enjoy as much as I can without guilt. However, this

A cluster of ruins are exposed by slow erosion in northern Baghdad. During OIF II soldiers could not stop to find out the origin or the age of the ruins.

absurdity can motivate me to pray for those who are in the line of fire tonight.

Because the list has grown so much I am anxious about sending anything out. Every time I hit the send button (on purpose) I cringe at the thought of what people might think. Have I gone too far on some point or opinion? Have I made simple spelling or grammatical mistakes that make me look foolish? Have I established an opinion that I will have to live with the rest of my life, and will my opinion change?

We all know that what we write represents us more than what we say because it goes so much farther than the people around you. This e-mail distribution system is a very powerful and wonderful tool that can be very dangerous at the same time.

I am aware that I will be judged by many for what I write in these e-mails and this is rather intimidating to me. Now a proverb of the bible says that since we are judged by our words so much that a good man shouldn't talk too much. Those of you who know me know that I struggle with the limiting of my verbose speech.

There is another problem here and that is it is now my occupation to inform people. I am part of a 24-soldier unit that has the mission of making sure the information flows to and from the soldiers. Furthermore I have this gift handed to me to write lengthy e-mails that you all seem to like very much.

Perhaps it's a divine calling or just a gifting. This leads to one possible conclusion and that is if one has to inform with speech or in writing we should be very careful about what we say or write. And even more careful about pushing that tiny little icon with the disc on it that means

save and not the one right next to it that says send.

For tonight's topic I want to expound on something I wrote about yesterday.

I wrote that the 1st Cavalry Division was turning up the heat, or in other words, fighting more aggressively and maybe insinuated that the 1st Armor Division had not. I want to explain what 1st Armored Division had been trying to accomplish as it was nearing what was supposed to be the end of it's

Above: Guard tower that stands sentinel outside the Water Palace was no match for the American Bradley Fighting Vehicle or the tanks that led the fight into Iraq. Below: There was a small building on it's own island. I referred to this as the Mother In-Law Villa.

time here in Iraq.

The guidance from higher at the time was to begin turning the city over to the Baghdad people and the army was supposed to be playing a lesser and lesser role in the city of Baghdad. 1st Armored Division had a mission called "Outside Looking In," in which the army was moving from many forward operating bases

Farmers carry out their business with horse drawn carts all over Baghdad. Baghdad was always an agricultural city and with the advent of the fuel distribution crisis in Baghdad during OIF II, many farmers found it more convenient to use grass powered vehicles rather than gas powered vehicles. Yes, insurgents used a donkey cart to launch a rocket attack against US forces destroying the animal.

(FOBs) inside the city, to 8 large ones outside the city. The mission was supposed to make the transition from being an occupier providing all the security and control to one of helping the Iraqi police and defense forces only when needed. The 1st Armored Division had scaled back it's patrolling efforts to some degree in order to accommodate this.

As 1st Cavalry came on board they began to patrol the rougher neighborhoods where the anti-coalition forces were recruiting from the impoverished and criminal element of the city. Shortly after their arrival, the incident at Falluja in which four American civilian workers were burned and mutilated, kicked off the current battle there. Moqtada al-Sadr couldn't stand the presence of 1st Cavalry soldiers in his

neighborhood and heated up his campaign until the army shut his printing press down. This sparked the uprising of

the Mehdi militia which has moved to An Najaf and Al Kut south of Baghdad.

The intensified fighting

changed everything and we went from a path that was supposed to lead us to a role of observation and intervention, to a path of aggressive warring against small militias numbering in the thousands each in two different regions. With the new intense fighting came the need for a new approach to the intensity of our fight. Not surprisingly the Texas-based soldiers have come out fighting with guns blazing.

I earnestly believe that 1st Cavalry soldiers at all levels have taken the fight to the enemy in a much more offensive way than was previously necessary. In so doing the cavalry has amassed a higher then expected amount of casualties and the numbers are expected to climb and surpass the previous unit by a lot.

How should we fight? Are

21

Humvee in front of hotel in downtown Baghdad. The statue represents post-modern art while the Humvee represents post military art.

we going to take the lesser aggressive and belligerent path of patrolling less and hoping things work out as we back step out of Baghdad? This will in no doubt lessen the amount of casualties for our side, but will it accomplish the mission and purpose for being here? I don't think so. The aggressive fighting style that the cavalry brings with it definitely has made a big impact. The Mehdi militia that was dominant in eastern Baghdad either died in place or ran south to regroup in Karbala and An Najaf. It cost us dearly from our perspective, but the Cavalry really put a hurt on them.

It will be interesting to see how the near future pans out. Whatever happens I hope we reduce the number of our enemy by a lot over the next few days.

May 01, 2004

Thanks for all the letters sent back. It is always good to hear from the home front. Each and everyone of those e-mails means a lot to me. The Internet has been so sporadic in connectivity that I haven't been able to attach pictures so this e-mail grew to the point that I am going to send it out in two parts.

NEWS FROM THE WAR FRONT: The supply lines are all back up and running just fine. The mail trucks, water trucks and trucks that pump out the porto-potties are all arriving just fine. There was a week there after the insurgent uprising where we had shortages and yes that included a place to go potty in some of the more remote locations.

The weather here fluctuates a lot as there isn't a single speed bump between here and Israel to hold the wind back. Two days ago it was a humid 100-ish degrees depending on which thermometer you referred to. Yesterday it was overcast

Above: The Tigris River runs through Baghdad, Iraq as seen from the helicopter.

and barely 80 degrees. The windstorms are kicking up the dust here tonight and it's pretty ugly out there. Today we had the thunderstorms arrive. Golf ball size hail has been falling intermittently between torrential downpours. It was really impressive tonight.

Construction is booming everywhere here in Baghdad. Every month some new major building or feature is completed and the standard of living takes a quantum leap for the better. In March our home trailers were built and finalized and we were able to move from the tents at the Airport. In April the dining facility opened up and we no longer had to walk over two miles round trip to eat a meal. Next month the new gym and the new shopping store called the PX should be done and within walking distance. The month after that the new building where I will work

Farm horses wait to be hitched in the early morning hours in southeastern Baghdad.

for the remaining time here will be done and that will be a huge improvement.

It is absolutely amazing how the government and the general level of leadership is taking care of soldiers better than ever and making life better as quickly as possible. Their commitment to health and welfare along with soldier morale shows, and is not just words in a speech,

but dollars on the table. This has all come at a very shiny dime, I'm sure. It is good to be in the US military, as compared to other militaries, and our own in the not so distant past.

The following is a lengthy discourse on the never ending debate between spending money on soldiers or not. I think this topic is important for citizens to know.

SOLDIER WELFARE AND MILITARY READINESS:

This is an enormous topic that is difficult to cover and quite boring for a non-military person like most of you to take in, but I think that it is the most important thing I will probably write about in these letters to you all.

The topic of how much to spend on soldier amenities and benefits is talked about all over Washington and usually sparks heated debate throughout the military. This topic has escaped the media as it is too much into the nuts and bolts of how the military works, but in reading this you will become an informed citizen and able to cast a much more responsible vote. I really think that the civilian audience out there needs to be aware of these issues because it eats up the lion's share of the defense budget. First I need to define some key words that the military likes to use.

READINESS: This is the overall ability for the military to go to fight anywhere in the world and take on any enemy at anytime. This concept of readiness applies to every echelon of the military from the Department of Defense, branches of service, division (about 17,000 soldiers) down to the com-

Due to poor drainage throughout the region, ponding waters permeate the local neighborhoods in every part of Baghdad after rains of spring and fall. Baghdad smelled of rotting organic matter at the onset of each rainy season and like rotten eggs at the end of the season as the ponded water used up available oxygen and the water became reduced.

panies (about 100 soldiers) and right down to Private Joe Snuffy being trained up, fully qualified to do his or her job and personally ready to deploy.

THE ALL VOLUNTEER MILITARY: This is the paradigm the US military exists in today and is completely unique to anything else in the world.

When the army transitioned into an all volunteer fighting force back in the 70s to do away with the unpopular draft, it created a problem that no general had ever had to face before: how to get enough young people to volunteer to maintain a military large enough to take care of the mission? Paychecks, benefits, retirement, college assistance and enlistment bonuses became the tools that American generals had to rely on without conscripted soldiers.

QUALITY OF THE FORCE: This is a difficult term to define with words and also a touchy subject because the truth is not always pretty as some of us would like it to be.

It refers to the overall qual-ity and caliber of soldiers that the military is able to recruit, both into the enlisted and officer ranks. It also refers to the caliber of military service members that the military branches of service are able to retain for long term service. This concept covers the overall natural born and developed abilities and state of being for individual soldiers that collectively make up military as a whole.

All branches of service have been striving to raise the level of quality of recruit into their branch, and then retain that soldier/sailor/ma-rine/airman for a long time. With the end of the draft in 1976, it has been gener-ally believed that the army has recruited and subsisted on stereotypically poor young people without bright futures. This was a huge improvement over conscript soldiers, so much so that many other militaries have been trying to transition to the same volunteer system.

The army learned that they could improve the quality of soldier coming in by offering better incentives such as bet-ter living conditions, college benefits and large entrance bonuses to entice young people to make the commit-ment. This greatly increased the "Readiness" of the army. Better quality trigger pullers

Above: A neighborhood west of Baghdad in the Abu Ghraib village near the infamous prison. Below: A neighborhood in southern Baghdad after a rainstorm.

create less problems for leadership, because disciplining of soldiers who don't want to be here or play well with others can be the biggest tax on the time and energy of both the NCO (sergeants) and the officer corps.

RETENTION: Getting as many soldiers as possible to stay in longer increases the average overall experience of soldiers in the military, decreases the burden to recruit new soldiers and increases the number of soldiers in each rank category competing for promotion.

The latter is the biggest payoff by far in my humble opinion because it increases the number of soldiers for the army to choose from to promote to the next higher level and directly increases the caliber of leadership.

The quality of leadership in the military, particularly with the sergeants corps, is what generals point to for our overwhelming success on the battlefield, citing the high-tech weaponry as only the tools of the trade that amplify the leadership's ability to capitalize on the enemies

deficiencies, rather than the source of victory itself.

A big problem with retention is after a major military conflict, a large number of soldiers go away, due to the horrible stresses that deployment and battle put on soldiers and their lives. The stresses that are put directly on the individual soldier are fatigue, sleep deprivation, diarrhea, exposure to the weather and the like.

The indirect stresses from deployment on soldiers' lives such as the stress on marriage from separation, paying bills, missing baby's first steps and such. We usually expect a mass exodus of about 20-25% of personnel to get out of the army after

The military invested heavily in comfort items such as these trailers which could be configured from six soldiers to a trailer to two fieldgrade officers or sergeant majors per trailer. These huts made all the difference in the world and moral beneffitted greatly during the Yearlong tour of duty. Left: The author next to his trailer. Below: The room of the author.

a major deployment. This is because many young people are enticed into the military for the enticements and not for the service.

SOMETHING IS DIFFERENT ABOUT THIS DEPLOYMENT: What happened? I'm being treated well by people and my living conditions are incredible compared to the recent past. What's going on? The views of the citizens towards soldiers and the military have changed so drastically over the past 13 years since Gulf War I. What happened? The army is treating me well and trying to make life better. This is not the army I joined, thank God.

When this war kicked off after 9-11 the president announced that this war would be a long one, fought all over the world. Fought continuously night and day. In one speech I can remember the president talked about what

a challenge this would be on the military and what a huge burden it would be on the reserves because we would have such a prominent roll.

Everyone, and I mean everyone jumped on the flag waving bandwagon and supported the troops. This put an enormous pressure on the politicians to show that they cared about the troops. Nothing is more noticeable than a voting record during an election year. I swear they must have come up with so many resolutions just so they could all show that they had voted for the American soldier.

The military didn't want to go through another fall out like they did after Gulf War I. The attrition really hurt the military. Everybody in the military blamed Clinton for the woes, and there was definitely some truth about that, but the lion's share was the recoil from lengthy deployments.

Above: A Russian motorcycle with side car was one of the many remnants left behind by the former Iraqi military. Saddam Hussein and his war machine purchased almost everything from factories in Russia. Motorcycle enthusiasts from the US found this and restored it to working condition.

The first trip outside the wire with the G-5 section was to northern Baghdad for a meeting with a high ranking sheik. I walked around and visited the soldiers on perimeter security. I saw an old man watching the women work in the fields near the Tigris River (Upper Left). He motioned me down to him. Like many other soldiers I had to decide whether or not to take the chance. I did and was rewarded with a three hour conversation with a man who couldn't speak a word of english, nor could I speak a word of his language. He first offered me a glass of cold water. I thought hard about the risk and then I drank the wonderful cold clear water. It tasted so good on that hot day. He then told his son to take cold cans of Orange Crush to the soldiers out on security (Lower Left). Later in the afternoon he sent his grandson (Right) to give cold clean water to the same soldiers out on security.

These deployments and these wars are the reason we have a military to begin with. That's our job. The military definitely spent some time thinking about the things that could be done to make soldiers' lifes better during deployment.

It's obvious that the leadership of both military generals and the government have put an enormous amount of resources into the standard of living for soldiers while they are on deployment.

Here is what you all need to know. The senators vote for the funding for all these incentives, benefits, salaries, quality of food, quality of housing, college benefits, etc.. etc... These benefits cost an enormous amount for the army, which is typically 10 times as large as the Air Force and bigger than all other branches combined. (I don't know if that last fact is true)

Many think that spending money in these areas fills our ranks with people who really don't want to go to war or serve their country. To them I ask, "Did the draft fill the ranks with people who wanted to go to war? There are many politicians and officers who regret diverting so much money away from ships and bullets to college funds and newer hospitals, but this is what is necessary to recruit and retain higher caliber soldiers.

These benefits are a huge drain away from what the more hard-headed generals who think like Archie Bunker would like to spend their budget on. Some of their arguments are legitimate, but they have forgotten, or never knew what the morale in Vietnam was like with all the problem children who didn't want to be there.

The buzzwords and phrases that I've heard is "spending money only on those things that help with near and long term readiness." That is to say they only want to have benefits that lead to a more "ready" military.

What this means is if they could spend money on something that makes soldiers' lives much better but will not cause them to reenlist, then they don't want to spend the money. That's the bottom line for many decision makers. Does budgeting for soldier welfare give us the desired results down the road?

Above: The author smoking a cigar in the back of an up-armored Humvee sitting on a chair that was part of the furniture from one of Hussein's palaces.

The answer is yes. The noted retention that is being reported is that the soldiers returning from war are planning on reenlisting and staying. I don't know how truthful that is but we can watch the numbers change over the next two to five years. It took five years for the full effect of Gulf War I to take affect, with the help of former President Clinton's draw down of the military in the early to mid nineties.

There is a point of limited return on each benefit and like businessmen trying to pinch out a profit, the decision makers have to pinch out their budgets to get the maximum effect. Most of the arguing going on is over how much and where to focus the financial efforts for readiness and retention related spending.

What gives the military, and hence the taxpayers, the most bang for their buck? Would spending the enormous money it would take so soldiers had hot tubs available to them be

nice for us here in Baghdad? Yes it would be, but would that cause retention and readiness to go up? It proba-bly wouldn't much at all and certainly not to the point that it is worth the cost.

The generals and the deci-sion makers are trying to ap-ply the concept of "Invisible Hand" from economics and spend money only on those things that produce a mea-surable impact on retention.

Have we gone overboard on the "we support our troops"?

No one in the military is openly going to admit to this, but people need to start asking this question. It is important to note that for an educat-ed voting citizen, that jumping on the bandwag-on and wav-ing the flag and scream-ing for more benefits is not neces-sarily what's best for you the taxpayers and certainly not what's best for the military as a whole.

This is unbelievable to have it this good in a theater of operation. The trailers, which hold from two field grade officers to six junior enlisted, depending on how they are configured, cost about $25,000 each. Will they make a difference in the short and long run for morale and welfare, and thus make an impact on retention and overall readiness? Absolutely yes in my humble opinion. The other day it was a really humid 104 degrees outside and I was sleeping inside a

Above and next two Pages: The slums north of Baghdad had homes made from rubbish in which people lived with their farm animals. The photo of the little girl running barefoot through the slums initiated a lot of sympathetic responses from the recipients of these e-mails. The people living in these slums were clearly used to soldiers giving them water and food.

closed container that was reasonably cool. Tonight we got hammered with golf ball size hail and torrential downpours, and I am perfectly warm and dry.

When they talk about defense spending and these topics in the news, particularly the topic of salary, which is the largest single expense in the Department of Defense, and education being a distant second, you will be more informed of why they are such big topics, and maybe you can vote for senators and see through their smoke screens of care and concern for the American soldier better.

Above and Below: The slums of northern Baghdad were home to some of the most destitute Iraqis who lived in shacks with their animals. Note the little girl running barefoot back to her dwelling.

May 4, 2004

On the war front today we have been arresting tens of bad guys with no deaths to American soldiers. The polls are out and the Iraqi people are glad we invaded, but don't think we had a right to invade. They think they're somewhat better off than last year, have a great deal of hope for a much better life this coming year and don't trust each other or their own Iraqi institutions. Very interesting.

The horrible incident with the pictures of the tortured prisoners is way over blown. Most Iraqis I doubt care about how we treat the criminals from the past regime. The detainees in Abu Ghraib prison are still alive, but their victims are not. I've met Iraqi people who are appalled at how well the detainees are getting treated in prison with AC and clean water and running toilets. Most Iraqi people don't have these things.

May 07, 2004
A Day Outside the Wire

Little has changed since last night. Let me see. I received my new tennis shoes in the mail today. That was exciting. I almost bought a camera but have decided not to for now. Just couldn't stand the thought of that much money over the Internet. I received a ton of e-mails from you all yesterday. I have no idea what happened but everybody had time and the notion to write on the same day. Please keep it up.

A DAY OUTSIDE THE WIRE: Miraculously I was able to get some days off and so I volunteered to go out on a convoy with the civil affairs group to the very north of Baghdad. The convoy took off and I was locked and loaded riding in a Humvee without any

doors. It was really cool to race around Baghdad on the highways hanging half out the door with loaded M-16. There is a certain adrenalin rush to it. I was looking at all the sites and people while keeping an eye out for anyone pointing a weapon at us.

A lieutenant, also from the night shift here at the head puzzle palace, had also volunteered to go. He was standing up in the same Humvee as I was riding in behind the machinegun they have mounted on a pedestal back there. We were traveling north when he screamed "RPG". That stands for rocket propelled grenade and is the main weapon that the enemy is taking out soft-skinned vehicles with. The watchful lieutenant was able to spot 4 RPGs leaning up against the back wall of an automotive shop with the two main doors wide open. We pulled the convoy of Humvees around and went

and all the men sat down and began to talk through an interpreter. They were negotiating things I cannot talk about.

I left the shack and walked around to all the perimeter guards to take pictures under the auspices that I was with the public affairs group and needed to get an article out of this "day outside the wire." Some of the soldiers had taken up positions along the bulwark on the dike along the banks of the Tigris River. When I went out to visit them I saw several women working in the fields inside the dike. I saw an old man watching them. He waved to me and I shouted in Arabic hello. I think that at the time that was probably the only word I knew. That was enough and the man was waving me over to see him. I was surrounded by soldiers with machineguns so I went over to see him. He insisted on giving me his seat and visiting with me. I was apprehensive of course and was very careful not to let my guard down and was only 100 feet from three armed soldiers.

We were sitting under a tree in the shade. He insisted that his son go to get some ice-cold orange juice and give it to me and the soldiers out on

Above and Below Right: The slums north of Baghdad were not only a dumping ground for the city's rubbish, but also the lack of vegetation and shade made for blistering temperatures and uneven heat convection caused "Dust Devils", rotating gusts of wind that look like small tornados. These strong winds blew constantly, moving the dust and trash around.

back. The lieutenant colonel that was with us insisted that we report the RPGs and drive on, because his meetings with several sheiks that day was our mission and reason for living. So we didn't attack and arrest, we just called in a grid coordinate and drove on. This made a lot of people mad.

When we got to the northern Forward Operating Base (FOB) on the edge of the Tigris River, we linked up with a handful of soldiers and interpreters and walked outside a small gate in the back side of the wall. We were all led to a small one room shack. The lieutenant colonel and a couple of majors went

inside and the rest of us pulled security. Nobody had any idea what was going on that day. None of the soldiers and certainly not myself, had been informed as to the purpose of the meeting that was about to take place. A sheik entered with his entourage. I could see that a banquet had been set in this little shack

Left: These two young boys came out to the convoy expecting water and food. They were too clean-cut and sharp looking to be living in the slums. It is likely that they saw the US patrols stopping daily if not hourly and decided to walk across the highway from a nearby development. Posing as slums dwellers is hardly a crime, but it did take away from those who really were living in the slums. Right: A dust devil kicks up the trash and dust adding to the miserable conditions in the slums.

perimeter guard. I took some photographs of the unexpected act of goodwill along with some more photographs of the old man and myself. Showing the man and his son the photographs on the back of my digital camera opened things up even more. Soon we were joined by his 14 year old grandson who spoke a little English.

I visited with the old man for over three hours. This was quite amazing as we didn't speak hardly any of each other's language. I really missed not being able to communicate with others from other lands.

What I was able to ascertain was that this very affluent area was a Shia area that had been heavily plundered by the Hussein regime. He and his friends are all part of a tribe, to whom the sheik was the leader of. He was very pro-American and wanted to shoot Moqtada al-Sadr. He was a farmer, although I can't imagine such a small farm being enough to support anyone. The 14 year old boy liked soccer, was in the 7th grade and had a Play Station II. He was a well dressed, well behaved and obviously very well raised young man who was probably very bright comparatively for his age.

After that incredible serendipitous experience I left with the convoy and headed south where we saw that the RPGs seen earlier were no longer in the same building. Hopefully the good guys came and got them. We kept on going down to the Green Zone, which is the central hub of all that goes on for coalition forces in a very well protected part of Baghdad for another meeting for the colonel. We spotted some people on a distant building that looked like they were taking up sniper positions, but they were too far

to tell for sure. After the meeting it was about 1630 hours, or 4:30 in the afternoon. We all walked to one of the fancy hotels of the old regime and had dinner at the restaurant there. It was fantastic. We then headed back to home. It had been an exhausting day and I was really tired after that.

___

May 08, 2004

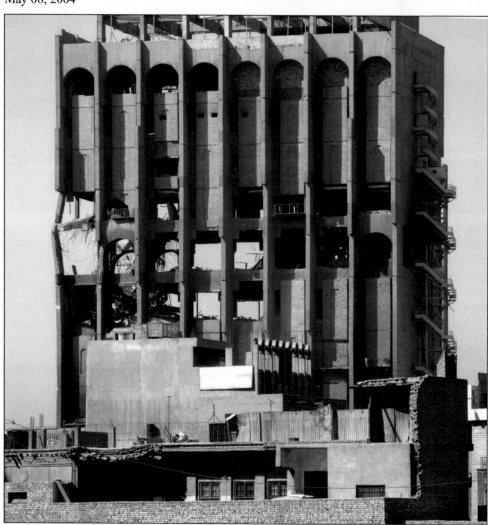

One of the many communications buildings in downtown Baghdad that was repeatedly hit by missiles and smart bombs during the "Shock and Awe" attack designed to decapitate the leadership.

From my older sister Linda Atkins: Tim;

Regarding the pictures and stories of torture by our military, can you comment on military mentality, war mentality? I asked Rick last night if things like this happen in every war, even going back to the wars of the Old Testa-

ment. And do you think war just brings out the very worst in us as humans no matter the cause of war? Also, If torture is the normal means of getting information, or whatever, why are there not laws about photographs of such events? I think average Joe citizen who supports the war and the troops does NOT want to know and see

these things.

Linda;

These are difficult questions to be sure. The subject of the evil that lies inside every human being and how it manifests itself in different situations is a problem that many people much more apt than myself have tried

to explain. My opinions are not going to be as credible as many others in the field of Military Intelligence (MI), but I can write a few words on the subject with regard to the latest scandal and the military community, because I have received some rudimentary training and education from the US military with regard to interrogation

and exploiting detainees for information. I have also received the training in the Laws of War and the Geneva Convention as well.

SOME BASICS ABOUT INTERROGATION: All these things I have talked about have been in articles or covered by documentaries that have aired publicly.

First of all, the US Military does not condone the use of torture of any kind. The arguments are all about what do you define as torture. If you ask ten different people you will get ten different answers. Here are some of the things I can say about the matter.

The first principle of interrogation is that most people who are taken captive by an enemy force love to talk. The police in America all say the same thing about arresting criminals. As soon as you capture someone just ask them to tell you information and more times than not, the individual will just start talking about things you never would have thought to ask about. The statistics I heard are that in WWII when Americans discovered this phenomenon, 70% of all Anglo-Saxons will just tell you everything without any prodding. Japanese captured in WWII had something along the lines of 50% who would talk without even being asked. Keep in mind I have never seen these statistics in writing. It has been shown through numerous cases that all other races of people fall in between these two statistics somewhere.

With that said, we are encountering more resistance among the Arabs over here and that is strongly attributed to the detainees in this case being rallied around a religious cause versus being conscripted fighters for a government they didn't like. The more you believe in your cause the more likely you are to resist the temptation to talk openly.

This first basic principle is the foremost taught by the United States. There is no need for torture of any kind on the battlefield.

It was also discovered early on that information gained through any means other than voluntary confession yielded the most inaccurate information.

I have spoken with several cops who have told me that easy arrests come from just walking up to an individual who looks like they are involved in crime and asking them if it's OK to search them or their car. The answer is almost always yes, or after arresting them they simply ask them, did you do this or that, and they often get an

A poor neighborhood in southeastern Baghdad.

Major General Chiarelli's coin that he would give out to individuals who deserved merit. This particular coin was presented to an Iraqi security agent who had been attacked with bombs twice by insurgents at his house and still came to work each day. No, I never received a coin.

Young boys play soccer on a field that was once a battlefield. Many battalions carried out these civil affairs type projects called "Battle field to Soccer Field" as a publicity stunt to humiliate the enemy and to deny them from using the same familiar areas for further attacks. Below: A young man waves while he watches two donkey carts. This was a very common sight in southern Baghdad where agriculture was a way of life.

31

Above: Farm boys ride with the sheep in the back of a typical farm truck called a Bongo Truck. The photo shows typical reaction to an American soldier with a large black camera in that some are enthusiastic to have their picture taken while others defiantly do not want to be photographed. This photo was taken barely inside the northern city limits near Baghdad Island. Right: A young girl makes a dangerous living in the difficult and austere times during the summer of 2004, by selling cigarettes in the middle of one of the busiest road intersections in the downtown area. Below: A young boy is excited to pose for the camera as the convoy passes by. It was rare to see young boys in the "Man Dress" and much more common to see them in modern western style clothing. The photo was taken in western Baghdad's Al Mansoor district where many wealthy people who were the movers and shakers from the old regime live.

answer that they can follow up on.

Everything I have read on extracting information from POWs strongly relies on fear. Fear is the number one tool that an interrogator has at his or her disposal.

Think how afraid a person must be when they are captured by an invading army of larger soldiers who look like American soldiers. All the body armor, the weapons

we carry and the vehicles we drive are all extremely intimidating.

There is an inherent fear factor when an enemy soldier is taken out of his element and put in an incredibly scary environment that is filled with the "fear of the unknown." Some POWs will go into shock or even have a heart attack over the fear factor alone.

Those are the basics of what the military intelligence community has to work with. In general, torture yields little information of value, but results in much greater control of those in custody and provides a deterrent for those who are still free to fight. The fear of torture and murder is being used against the employees of coalition forces over here and it is working.

HOW THE INCIDENT IS

BEING HANDLED: Get dirty early. This is a phrase that the army uses a lot. It means when you find that your institution is in the wrong about something then you need to come out and admit it as soon as possible. The sooner you admit to it and get it out in the open the easier it is to deal with.

This was done. I have been hearing about the court-martial of these individuals for the last four months. I have heard about them on the Armed Forces Radio and read about them in the military newspapers. So something bad happened and the army released the news, and now much later this scandal has erupted into something that could potentially cost Mr. Rumsfeld his job. What happened?

Pictures! That's what happened. Before all this, the information was out there and readily available to the media but you all never heard anything about it, because there weren't any pictures. Pictures! Loud, provocative, scandalous pictures that are so entertaining to see. They captivate your attention and they hold it for days, weeks, months as the advertising dollars roll in and keep on rolling in to the civilian media outlets.

The more the media embellishes on this topic, and it will for many weeks, because that's how long these pictures will hold the world's attention for, the more money the corporations make and the more fame and notoriety the reporters can gain at the expense of the army's credibility.

This is true for both the conservative and liberal media out there but there is a huge gain in those who are opposed to the current president. Theirs is the goal to exploit this incident and embellish it for all it's worth for the purpose of damaging the president's chances at re-election. That is a no brainer.

There are many different things I could say on this manner but I am tired of writing and must get to work so I can write many reports on what is happening and going on in the Baghdad area. By the way there is a lot of good news tonight, of which I can tell you nothing, but we captured somebody tonight along with a lot of explo-sives. Shhhhh!

As for the questions my sister asked about the mentality and brutality of people in the military during times of war. I really can't talk about that much, because I am not an expert in psychology.

One sad thing I can say: I earnestly believe that these acts of brutality and much worse are taking place all over the world at all times. In every small town in America there is some older brother who is brutally abusing a little sister or a younger brother, gangs across Amer-ica are kidnapping each other, raping, torturing and castrating each other, people are murdered slowly and painfully all the time, chil-dren are either kidnapped or sold by their parents into the sex slave trade where they must be raped repeatedly and brainwashed in a hideous manner so they will perform as they are required, innocent people are rotting in jails all over the world while their accusers confiscate their belong-ings, and the list goes on and on.

I'm sor-ry but war doesn't bring this out in people. War just affords people the opportunity to allow the evil within them to manifest itself in ways that it other-wise could not.

Life in a fallen world sucks. To-night's topic was not very encouraging I'm afraid, and there is so much more to be said along these lines, but I am tired and must get back to work.

The once stalwart columns of the former Iraqi Ministry of Defense still stand above the ruins and rubble that resulted from the "Shock and Awe" that preceded the invasion. The once formidable structure that corresponded to the Pentagon in the US was the site of decision making and planning that terrorized the entire Middle East. The view above and next page are of the outside corridor that gave the building a grand and imposing demeanor of seriousness.

May 18, 2004

Well the kindergarten trip didn't turn out that well. They've had lots of American soldiers come to that school bringing toys and candy. We didn't bring anything but boring school supplies.

It was a really horrible day

for me as I was sick with the Baghdad crud. It was better than just returning to my room and staring at the walls. The camera worked so poorly that I have bought two new cameras, one of them is on order.

Tonight's topic is Humvees. The Humvees over here are taking a pretty good beating and when they return they are going to be quite a maintenance nightmare for the future soldiers. We're starting to see some armored Humvee kits arrive.

The army has taken to mounting a pedestal in the back of the Humvee to mount the heavier machineguns on such as the M2 0.50 cal anti-armor machinegun and the M240 7.62mm machinegun that are too heavy and powerful for an individual to hold. However, the soldiers like mounting their much smaller M249 handheld SAW 5.56mm machineguns on the pedestal mounts.

The soldiers are exposed to whatever happens with the doors off. This is what has so many people outraged back in the United States. The armor kits are so few and the arrival of new completely armored Humvees is so slow that some people will be driving with no doors on the Humvee for quite some time.

I have no complaints here about the lack of armament on the Humvees. With all the technological innovations over the past 30 years that have given us superior edge in the global fight, this Humvee oversight, and it is a legitimate oversight on the part of Department of Defense, is grossly overshadowed by all the "we guessed rights" and the "I told you so's" of the past six presidents and their entourage of decision makers.

One legitimate complaint

The imposing columns of the old Iraqi Ministry of Defense building still standing after the initial "Shock and Awe" attack. Below: the main entrance was hit hardest by the missile attack. This building actually was well built compared to the palaces and was structurally sound enough to allow use by soldiers during the early part of the occupation.

that I have always had is over there where you all are. If there is no lobby, then there is no push in Congress to field new equipment.

The fastest way to make sure new equipment is on the battlefield and working correctly is to make sure that someone is making billions of dollars of profit off of it.

There is no real push to get the badly needed armored kits over here. If Kellogg Brown and Root were in the mix and lots of profit were to be had then they'd be here by now.

June 12th 2004

Distributed Joke
Why Did the Chicken Cross the Road?

Coalition Provisional Authority: The fact that the Iraqi chicken crossed the road definitively demonstrates that decision-making authority has been transferred to the chicken well in advance of the scheduled June 30th transition of power. From now on the chicken is responsible for its own decisions.

Halliburton: We were asked to help the chicken cross the road. Given the inherent risk of road crossing and the rarity of chickens, this operation will only cost the US government $326,004.

Moqtada al-Sadr: The chicken was a tool of the evil coalition and will be killed.

US Army military police: We were directed to prepare the chicken to cross the road. As part of these preparations, individual soldiers ran over the chicken repeatedly and then plucked the chicken. We deeply regret the occurrence of any chicken rights violations.

Peshmerga: The chicken crossed the road, and will continue to cross the road, to show its independence and

Left: A typical scene at an Iraqi school when soldiers come to visit. Most of the schools had been damaged during the invasion, because the old regime used to hide large quantities of ammunition and weapons in schools. The US Army was paying to have each and every school renovated. The children had come to expect toys, games and candy. The soldiers originally came up with the idea of sending home for shoes for the kids. This eventually turned into a sponsored program. Soldiers also started having school supplies sent to them so that they could deliver them to the needy schools that had been badly neglected. This eventually turned into Operation Backpack and Operation Pencil. There was some rejection by some students at many schools and soldiers who visited schools in Sunni areas were unwelcome. Middle: Sergeant Smith signs his autograph for some young boys in western Baghdad. It's hard to tell how much of an impact these acts of goodwill will have on the Iraqi people's opinion about us, but most soldiers believe that the future relations between America and Iraq have already been positively solidified in the children of Iraq.

to transport the weapons it needs to defend itself. However, in the future, to avoid problems, the chicken will be called a duck and will wear a plastic bill.

1st Cav: The chicken was not authorized to cross the road without displaying two forms of picture identification: Thus, the chicken was appropriately detained and searched in accordance with current SOPs. We apologize for any embarrassment to the chicken. As a result of this unfortunate incident, the command has instituted a gender sensitivity training program and all future chicken searches will be conducted by female soldiers.

AI Jazeera: The chicken was forced to cross the road multiple times at gunpoint by a large group of occupation soldiers, according to eye-witnesses. The chicken was then fired upon intentionally, in yet another example of the abuse of innocent Iraqi chickens.

Special Forces: We cannot confirm any involvement in the chicken-road-crossing incident.

Translators: Chicken he cross street because bad she tangle regulation. Future chicken table against my request.

US Marine Corps: The chicken is dead.

Navy: The chicken upon crossing the road was painted and lashed to the curb.

Kerry: "The chicken crossed the road before it did not"

Baghdad Bob: The chicken never crossed the road! He is safe in Baghdad, miles from the marauding vehicles of the infidel! THERE IS NO ROAD!

USAF: "As you can see here in the target video, the bomb was locked onto the chicken... and there it goes... the chicken

Father and Son, Specialist and Sergeant Major Brown both served in the 1st Cav during OIF II and received much media attention.

In the summer of 2004 I began working with Iraqi and western media. The job was one that I had received no training or preparation for. I learned an enormous amount of information about the media industry and the world as a whole.

is still moving... still moving... and unfortunately passed out of the parameters of the guidance system so that the bomb completely missed it and hit the weasel instead. Gotta admit though, it's impressive footage..."

Found this one in my inbox tonight and I hope you all liked it.

June 13th, 2004

As I finished my shift on Monday morning the G-5 colonel I had gone out with before offered to take me on the day's convoy for two more meetings. I had two hours to kill. I got back to my trailer and found out I had to pick up some package at the mailroom so I went and it was the new camera I had ordered. I was now too excited to get the catnap I was hoping for and had just enough time to charge the batteries before leaving on the convoy.

We drove all the way from the southwest side of Baghdad to the northeast edge of the city where we went into a gated compound. I went into the meeting with the colonel. We met with a Sunni cleric. It was really fascinating. The three officers, myself included, went upstairs

where we met a group of people. It was very weird being in a room filled with Sunni fundamentalist Muslims and there being only three of us Americans. There

A horse drawn wagon pulls its way through heavy traffic.

were only two weapons in the room. My M-16 and the Arab guard with an AK-47 carbine. We met for an hour and discussed how they want us to give them money to rebuild their buildings and pay their clerics.

This was somewhat interesting. This Sunni cleric said that Shia Muslim clerics demand that their patrons give 20% to the mosques and they have been receiving money from the Shiites in Iran all these years of oppression from Hussein's Regime. The Sunni follow the

Koran which only requires 2.5% from the patrons, and there is no outside support, therefore the US should give the Sunni Clerics money. Makes perfect sense to me.

We drove somewhere downtown into some pretty rough neighborhoods and stopped at the really crowded part of town where the buildings were on the order of 10 stories high. This time we went into a building where an influential businessman was waiting for us. We went up about three stories of stairs. There were no lights in the building. It was pretty cool. We met with this manager of the "Family Business" for about an hour. He was smoking this really great smelling Cuban cigar. Oh

how I wanted him to offer us

a smoke.

He told us that just two days ago some terrorists tried to kill him. He was able to get away, but his sister-in-law was murdered. They had the funeral the day before. When he was asked about the kidnapping of a prominent business family's son he responded that not only did he know about it, he knew them well. According to this man, the kidnapping of children of affluent families is very common in Baghdad.

The army is trying to meet with this man and several others to come up with a plan for economic growth and development of Baghdad. It doesn't take a business conference to realize that we need to get rid of the bad guys more and open up the supply lines so that transportation of materials and goods can flow more freely and less expensively.

That meeting ended and we reversed our steps back to base. I caught a three hour nap and then went to work for my 12 hour shift. You would think that I would have slept like a log when I got off the next morning, but they keep turning the AC off in our little trailer courts so my room kept going over 100 degrees throughout the day and I could hardly sleep.

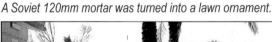

A Soviet 120mm mortar was turned into a lawn ornament.

It was the next day that I slept 9-10 hours. The melatonin is definitely helping, but it's not the miracle cure I had hoped for.

has really been doing a great job. We are very busy here trying to make Arab media press conferences take place so that the good news of new

The army celebrated it's 229th Birthday. 1st Cavalry Division had a division run around Camp Victory North. I am told that there were

will be replacing the three-star General Sanchez.

Things are continuing to slow down around here. The rebellions of late March that were mainly fought in April have all petered out and most of the bad guys are dead. The number of reported roadside bombs has decreased from 20-40 per 24hr day, when I first got here, down to 5-10 per 24hr day these past 10 days or so. This is a good thing. If you kill enough of the bad guys, people stop wanting to fight you.

Above: The 1st Cav Division is all about tradition. This is Trigger, the division mascot. Trigger is a plastic horse that rode over to Iraq in a conex on a ship. The saddle, bridle rifle and all other items on the horse were all presented to the 1st Cavalry Division by various units and individuals within the division. Soldiers gathered around Trigger to swear in for their reenlistments. Below: A typical sunset on Z Lake at my favorite cigar spot.

I was allowed a couple of nights off in which I only had to work about 3 hours each night to make sure that my replacement got the reports off and that they were done right. I actually went to church service for the first time since February 10th in Pullman. It was really a great service and a badly needed one. Oh the heathen and the pagan that I am. I should not have put that off for that length of time. I sure feel recharged now.

After church I went out with several friends to the palaces and to take photos with the new Sony camera that I really like so well. It was a great day until we got back to find the power was off and would be off for the next 12 hours. A backhoe had dug through the power cable and we were out in the heat. The temperature was around 110 the past couple of days. It's getting hotter. The hotbox of a room threw my sleep pattern off again, so I will be trying hard to stay awake tonight and will attempt to get back on track tomorrow.

I found some of the weight that I had lost. I was drinking all this flavored water, particularly flavored ice tea and then realized I was probably taking in 3 thousand calories a day. It'll come off quickly enough. I just got to drink water only

June 14, 2004

There has been a lot going on. The shop that I work for

sewage treatment plants gets out to the Arab population. I do believe that this little section at the Division Main is having a huge positive impact on the battlefield.

some really huge and fanciful cakes at the starting-finishing line. I wonder if that defeats the purpose.

The Military has announced that four-star General Casey

for a couple of days and the heat will take care of the rest.

Take care, and let me know what's going on in the real world.

June 16, 2004

I decided to share with you my responses to my nephew Andrew's e-mail. Andrew is very busy and yet he took the time to write his dearly loved uncle Tim. Isn't that nice and aren't you all feeling the guilt vibes? Needless to say I answered the questions in really sarcastic humor that I hope doesn't bother poor Andrew, particularly now that he is bigger than I am and still young (22ish I think).
--Hey Tim it's Andrew, I'm glad to hear that you'll be able to watch the Cougar football games. It's just too bad that they could never compete with the Wolverines University of Michigan Student).

Towards the end of OIF II there was an emergence of foreign militaries and equipment at Victory North (Later named Camp Liberty). Here are helicopters I never could identify.

+Dear Nephew; Dear, Dear, Sweet Nephew;
Clearly my sister did not raise you to be a nonsensi-cal waste of oxygen that you now appear to be, and I am sure that after this letter of correction I will never have

to hear such idiosyncratic rhetoric that displays the level of denial of reality that you obviously are living in.

A Blackhawk takes off from Pegasus Pad. This was the helicopter pad for Camp Victory North

I'm the crazy uncle of the family and you shall not usurp my undeniable sovereignty at this titled position with statements such as the aforementioned self-defaming sentences that crept forth from your fingertips. Go Cougs!! !
--If they play in the Rose Bowl, if Michigan isn't playing in the championship that is, we'll have to bet a beer on the game or something.
+If you want to blatantly give me a beer under such conditions, then why don't you just say, "Hey uncle Tim, why don't I just promise to buy you a beer the next time our two alma maters play each other." (I did not know that almamater was really two words alma mater, thanks spell-checker)
--Well there's a bunch of misc. questions on various things that I want to ask you about since I haven't talked to you in quite a while so it'll all be blended to-

gether without structure (I'd fail if I were turning this into a professor).
+That's Ok, I always wrote that way and turned it in anyhow and I got to take a few classes over because of it. It doesn't hurt that bad.
--It's good to hear that things are calming down around there. I'm looking forward to Grandpa's birthday gettogether, it's really too bad you can't make it. Are you going to try to call over that weekend?
+I'm afraid I'll probably miss his birthday, but that's OK. He's had so many of them I've attended too many as it is.
--I was wondering, do you have time to get target practice in with your M-16 and if so, where can you do it?
+Are you kidding the army is just now letting me run with sharp objects. By the time I retire I will be allowed to spell M-16 and that's about all. Actually there is a weapons range not far from here. I had fun shooting there and did quite well.
--My buddy's wife is in the

army band out there, she plays the french horn and sings, and she's going to be going around to different camps to play. Have you guys had the band come yet or are you expecting them to?
+Which band and what's her name? I have dealt with the 1st Cavalry Band a handful of times.
--I read what you said about the guy you met with that was smoking the Cuban cigar. I can see how you would've been anxious for him to ask if you wanted one. So can you guys smoke one as long as it's not on a military base?
+We can smoke the Cubans on base. They sell them here.
--My parents, Casey, and I are going up to Victoria in a month or so and last time I had a pretty good Cuban and I can't wait to try a couple more. Any suggestions? The last one I tried was an H. Upman.
+No I don't care for Cuban cigars at all, I think the Do-

Chaplain Johnson wanted to baptise soldiers so he went and found a large shipping crate in the motorpool. He lined it with plastic and asked the fire fighters to drive their engine by every Sunday morning and fill the make-shift baptismal with water so he could baptise right after service. He baptised often.

Above: 1st Cavalry Division Deputy Chaplain Major Johnson baptises a soldier outside the division chapel.

restaurants have a cigar menu on either the dessert menu or even on the back of the main dinner menu and

Below: The Praise and Worship Team led by many different believers throughout the year, warms up before a service at the division chapel. Chaplain, Lieutenant Colonel Moran, the division chaplain is seen tuning his guitar in the background while Corporal Jackson warmed up on the keyboard in preparation for Sunday service.

minicans and the Hondurans are better now and I don't like my money going into Fidel's pocket. No I can't send any Cuban cigars home to you. The cigars that I buy over here are Dominican and are very very good. I will sneak several hundred dollars worth home in my duffel bags.
--My parents said that when you came out to visit them that you tried to have a cigar in our tavern down by the water and they wouldn't allow it. It's funny out here on the west coast. Back in Michigan most of the nice

they usually have nice bars within the restaurant that you can smoke them in.

+The rest of America refers to the west coast as the "Left Coast". If it wasn't for the fact that the Pacific Northwest is so much better of a place to live, then I wouldn't live there I assure you. I miss the mountains and the micro-

different religions for every ship, air base and army division. The army often contracts out. Right now there is a huge shortage of Catholic priests and so the army is always hiring out for that.

--Well I ought to get going. I look forward to you coming back and maybe we could meet up for a cigar and a

people. It keeps me going and can snap me out of the blues sometime.

Tim

_____

June 20, 2004

From Dad:
--TIM TATE I just read

responses. Did you get to see the Lakers get beat up on by Detroit?

+I do too know what month your birthday is in. Its in July, now, as far as which day of the month it is.... I attended at least 18 of those birthdays. Yes I saw the Pistons whoop up on the Lakers. I was rootin' for whoever was playing the Lakers.

From Sheri:
--I just wanted to let you know I do enjoy your e-mails and continue to pray for your safe return home. I'm wondering two things. A while back you mentioned the armor plating that was being added to the vehicles. That was being done by a local Portland company. A friend of mine was scheduled to be there completing the project, (Jay Rose) and I'm curious as to whether it was successful. Secondly, being the sissy that I am, I heard about the HUGE spiders that were there. You have never mentioned anything about them. I thought (A) you were used to them or (B) they're not really THAT big or (C) they don't even exist.

Above and Below Right: The new Iraqi Government insisted on having a socialist fuel distribution system in which the government controls and subsidizes the cost of gasoline completely. A gallon of gas would cost 20 cents in Baghdad. The system was grossly incompetent and corrupt. The line of cars here disappears into the background and went forward nearly as far. People often waited 8 to 12 hours for the cheap gas. Tempers often flared and shootings and stabbings were common.

brew and the scotch.
--Do they have different services for different religions and branches of Christianity scheduled throughout the day on Sunday in the same building, or how does it work trying to fit in all of the different services? Do they just have a few chaplains that cover every type of service?

+The military tries to maintain different types of chaplains from every religion and denomination, but it is very difficult to recruit and train and retain chaplains in the

beer sometime (if we could find a place that allows us to smoke them). Well, take care.

Andrew

+Well you got your name right, now start rooting for the one correct team. Thanks for the note Andrew. I enjoyed answering all your questions. Hope you don't mind that I decided to share it with the rest of my family and friends or the sarcastic humor there. It means a lot to me to get e-mail from

your latest essay directed to Andrew. What do you mean you have attended too many of my birthdays "as it is"?? You have not been able to remember even what month it is, ever. Very good

+The up-armor kits did arrive and yes they have all been added and I can tell you that they make a difference for the units that patrol every day. However, whenever you add armor, whether it be to a vehicle or to the body, you decrease mobility and reaction speed. It is almost impossible for the soldiers riding inside to see the enemy let alone fire back and kill the attackers when they are attacked out on their patrols.

The spider you are referring to is the camel spider. Everything you have heard about them is true. I personally have seen three here. They grow to about 6.5 inches in diameter, can sprint short distances at 7 miles an hour, and can jump up four feet in the air. They are very aggressive and do attack people; however, they are non-venomous except for the germs and parasites that they may have in their mouths when they do bite. The rats pose much more of a threat to soldiers in the field, but their influence on the camps and bases that we now occupy has been greatly reduced.

From Uncle Jack:
--Hello, Tim; I enjoy hearing from you. I find your news items very interesting. One question I have is - did the policemen ever get their

badges they were supposed to get? Is the corruption still rampant in the Iraqi society?

+No the policemen still have not gotten their badges. You will notice in today's news that the Saudi Arabia

Al-Qaeda kidnappers posed as policemen. This is a standard tactic. The Police

uniforms cost about 7 dollars in Baghdad and the enemy is using this tactic almost daily to extort money from people. The reason that a badge is so important is that badges are difficult to counterfeit. You have to have some where-

with-all to make something like an official metallic badge. You never think about

these things in America, but in the 3rd world there is no way of telling if the guy who is ordering you around is really a police officer or not.

Yes the corruption is still very rampant. I do believe that the best we will ever see in Iraq is something like a well organized Mexico. I am told by someone who grew up here that Iraqi people used to be very morally conservative and if a young boy got caught stealing then the family would have to move to another neighborhood because of the disgrace. The only way to survive under Hussein and the Ba'ath party's rule was to become corrupt. We'll see over the next 10 years if the corruption goes away.

Now for what's going on around here. Geraldo Rivera has been in our area of operation for less then a week and was invited to leave because he lied to the leadership here too many times. He is asking

Above: The Color Guard of for the 2nd Battalion of the 5th Cavalry Regiment from 2nd Brigade Combat Team proudly display their battalion colors (Flag) during the ceremony honoring its heroes and soldiers who were injured during combat operations in the Spring of 2004.

to come back to our soldiers one more time, and he may get his way, but what a pain in the back side these celebrity journalists are.

I was able to take a small trip the other day and deliver brand new AK-47 assault rifles to the Iraqi police. That was interesting.

The story I did on the Sergeant Major Brown and his son both serving here in 1st Cavalry Division together is still the only one that I got published, and it's getting a lot of attention. They now want to do a live interview with the two of them on national TV because of the story I wrote. Go figure. I asked the Sergeant Major to make some phone calls for me and see if he could get me some more opportunities to cover soldiers in his son's unit, since they all know who I am. We'll see if I can make that happen sometime in the future.

The powers that be around here are talking about taking me off the night shift. I don't know if I want to go off of the night shift. I have a lot of freedom here that I won't

Above: Ceremonies honoring soldiers with medals and purple Hearts were common in the summer of 2004 following the uprisings in Falluja and Sadr City. Here the 2nd Brigade Combat Team is awarding medals to soldiers who were injured in western Baghdad while combating the Falluja fighters.

on the day shift. If I work on the day shift, then I'll have to deal with the people I work with and that just might ruin my career.

Well I better go. What kind of guilt trip should I lay on you all so I can get some more e-mails. Feel very, very, very guilty about how comfortable you all are right now and how all the brave American soldiers are suffering in unthinkable heat so you all can be safe and sound and drink beer, and drink scotch and.........

Please remember me and e-mail back once in a while.

———————————————

June 24, 2004

Tonight Geraldo came back after countless pleading and again he was a real pain in the backside. We have Dan Rather here now and soon Peter Jennings is coming.

The Iraqi President wanted to show his force so when he was mad at people parking on a street that they're not supposed to, he told everyone that Saddam wasn't anything and he took a baton and walked down and broke every window of every vehicle on the crowded street. The next day there were no cars parked outside his

office. Makes you wonder about this guy.

The Iraqi police are doing a much better job of fighting back and standing their ground. That's a good sign. The uprising this past 24 hours in which 85 people were killed is very small compared to the last one in April. There just aren't enough bad guys left to keep a fight going. The attacks and the frequency are always fluctuating indicating to me that there isn't a whole lot of different cells and organizations out there that are able to sustain the fight. We are winning.

Our MREs now come with coffee gum in which we can get our caffeine fix without brewing a cup. Yeah.

———————————————

June 29, 2004

I went with the convoy to deliver captured AK-47s to the Iraqi police. It was a very interesting trip. I met a

2nd Brigade Combat Team's Commander, Colonel Formica, pins awards on soldiers at Camp Black Jack.

lot of Iraqis there and they really liked Americans. I keep having mostly positive experiences with these people and so my views are obviously biased towards optimism. There are many soldiers, particularly in eastern Baghdad, that are not having the same warm and fuzzy experiences that I am. Some soldiers will probably come home disturbed and that's sad, but war is hell.

July 07, 2004
Hotter then....

I was able to get out and go with the civil affairs officer to central Baghdad. I attended a meeting with Major General Chiarelli and a Sunni Muslim leader. That was really interesting. I also was given about three hours to travel with the "Shadow Force" Personal Security Detachment. We went all over Baghdad.

The temperature is now over 100 degrees by 9:00 a.m.. The daily highs have been around 112 to 115 and still climbing. When I was riding around Baghdad, the sergeants had me stand up in the back next to the machinegunner so I could get better pictures. That was incredible. The 117 degree ambient air temperature at 55 mph was a real convection oven. The wind on my face and body was physically painful. I felt pain from the heat the entire trip. The metal on the Humvee was painfully hot to touch, so we all wore our gloves.

It was particularly taxing on me because I am not used to being out in the weather all day like the others and I had been up for about 17 hours by the time we took the trip. I had worked the night shift the night before and then went on the convoy.

Sheep are born, raised, spend their entire lives and then are herded off to market within the city limits of Baghdad. This city has never had sanitation or sewage treatment of any kind for all the livestock being farmed here.

A billboard advertising a career in the new Iraqi police and defense forces along a major highway. Notice that there are no bullet holes in this one. After a year in Baghdad. The defense forces such as the new Iraqi police and the Iraqi National Guard came a long way in both numbers, credibility and capabilities.

Posters and statues of Saddam Hussein were literally everywhere in Baghdad when coalition forces first entered. They were often destroyed by the Iraqis and sought after as war trophies by US soldiers. This one was immovable and soon became target practice, probably for Iraqis.

When the convoy was over that afternoon, I was able to get about three hours sleep before starting the next night shift. It was absolutely horrible the second night and absolutely worth it. Even though I was completely hung-over from dehydration (no alcohol, honest) the things I saw and photographed made it all worth the misery.

We skirted the side of Sadr City in eastern Baghdad. Less than half of the people waved back at me in these worst parts of Baghdad.

The little girl in the dump really got to me. The sergeants told me they were going to take me to some slums where people lived and built their homes out of the trash. I couldn't believe what I saw. Then this little girl comes running out of the barn/house bare-foot running over the trash. We gave them cold water and some candy. They all looked surprisingly healthy and the kids were handsome kids. It was really strange. I have no idea what their story was.

There are some bad politics going on here between the National Guardsmen and the Active Duty people. I am caught in the middle unfortunately. I am getting along with pretty much everyone on both sides. It is difficult for everyone to get along. I find mostly really good things to say about both sides. There is also some things that aren't so flattering to say about everyone on both sides.

I'm being told more and more that I will be coming off of night shift. I'll believe it when I see it, but I am now starting to look forward to it. I have now been doing this night shift battle captain job for four months. I can't wait to do something different.

I appreciate all your thoughts and prayers and concern for me.

Another surreal view of the sunset from the Al Fah Water Palace on a hot August summer evening.

July 09, 2004

The temperature is now above 100 degrees every day by 9:00 a.m. when I get off my night shift so running is out of the question. The humidity goes up every night trapping the heat in and it may be a while before we see anything starting with the number 8 again. It got all the way down to 90 degrees yesterday morning at 4:30 a.m. and it feels about 95 degrees now at 5:00 a.m. this morning. Enough bragging about how hot it is. I'm working in an air conditioned building. That's the only thing that matters. God bless the taxpayers.

Can't wait for the Cougs to start whoopin' tail this year. It's another 10-win season for sure. They're completely unranked again, but take my word for it that they and the Trojans are the teams to beat.

I was able to buy a Cougar flag and I had a lieutenant hang it up in the dining facility for me. It's right next to General Chiarelli's Husky flag. I'll take a picture of it and send that along sometime.

_____

July 14, 2004

I have been training the new lieutenant to take over my night job and she is doing absolutely wonderful. It's so much easier for her to come in here now that everything is built, everything is where it's supposed to be and all the systems are completed. It was a long drawn out process of one move and one improvement at a time. I also am doing a good job of training her. I didn't have much to go on and there really wasn't anyone who could train me or take the time to do so.

Everything keeps getting better. I took the LT to the big palace that you all have seen so many pictures of. I could look out from the third floor balcony and see the lights of Baghdad. It was absolutely unbelievable. There were absolutely no lights in Baghdad when we arrived. It may only be at 30% power but the city is coming to life. It really blew me away. It was such a day and night difference compared to March when we arrived here in Baghdad and stayed at the airport for one month.

If we can clean up this Mehdi militia in the next couple of months then this country will be a big success regard-

The sun sets behind the palaces on the lake near the Airport in southwestern Baghdad creating a surreal experience on a hot August evening. The water was particularly low that summer in 2004.

less of who gets elected. I am convinced of this.

July 18, 2004

I have been told that I come off of the night shift in two more days. I still can't believe it. There will be all sorts of adjustments that need to be made and I certainly hope that will go well. I am really looking forward to the changes. The lieutenant that is replacing me has been able to pick up on the night shift so fast, it made my head spin.

July 30, 2004

Yesterday was a long day with the NBC camera crew. They're a good bunch, as long as you don't mind what the NBC headquarters in New York does with their stuff. When you see the Olympics and they start showing cuts from soldiers and marines wishing the Olympiads the best of luck,

Another view from the upper floors of Saddam Hussein's personal hospital, looking out over the Tigris River where many wealthy people from the old regime lived and some still do. Behind the high rise apartments in the background is the Haifa Street area where so much fighting took place.

that was what I did yesterday. I helped arrange that and I escorted the NBC crew in and worked the whole media event from start to finish. That is my one feather in my cap for the week.

I also escorted an ABC camera crew around. I'll have to show the pictures of the pretty blond on that one. Martha somebody (Martha Raddatz) from ABC Nightline News. I gotta figure

out how to remember pretty women's names someday. There is no doubt why I am still a bachelor. When I dropped them off I got to see their quarters. Evidently they are staying in the three-star generals place. It was unbelievably huge and beautiful.

Today was 116 in the shade and I ran errands at noon for two hours and thought I was going to die. I bought a bicycle for getting around here. I can't wait for the weight room to re-open so I can get some decent workouts.

July 23, 2004

There has been an enormous amount of things happen to me since I got on day shift and I don't have a lot of time to write so here it goes as fast as I can. I was given two days off and on one of those days I went out on a convoy downtown. The colonel and I went into a meeting with two different sheiks, both of whom did not like

A soldier from the 3-82 Field Artillery pulls security as the Humvee rolls by on a night patrol in downtown Baghdad.

the US at all. The meeting was arranged by the Iraqi General for police. He had to bribe the men with weapons permits and other things under his control in order to get them to show up.

While we were meeting with the first sheik, the Iraqis in the room received a report from their intelligence indicating that this man was a known financier of terrorism. We let him go because we want the sheiks to continue to come and meet with us. What the Iraqi police did about the man, I don't know. They may have arrested him.

The second sheik was a real live wire. He was a feisty man and I really liked

him even though he clearly didn't want any soldiers in Iraq. He kept saying that all Americans will be great friends, but only after the military leaves. The doors to the side of the room opened up and there was a great feast for us. I gorged myself. The food was fantastic. After the meal the man was much more comfortable around us and was much more cooperative. We got some agreement from him for future coordination. That was a huge success story for all of us.

We later returned to central Baghdad where the colonel

left for a meeting. He came rushing out and informed us that an interpreter and friend of his had just got a phone call from his wife informing him that his house had just been bombed. The colonel wanted to take the convoy to his house and secure the neighborhood, mainly for a sign of support and to show the high ranking Iraqi official that we care. We did just that and the man lived in a gorgeous neighborhood. When we pulled into the maze of alleys to get to his house all the neighbors came out and gawked at us.

I had the big camera with me and the colonel kept telling me to get into the area where the bomb had been

and take pictures so I did. Soon I was taking pictures with the neighborhood kids looking at me and trying to talk to me. It was an absolutely gorgeous neighborhood. The houses were fantastic. Soon I was being motioned into the house by the colonel to take pictures of the damage done to the inside of the home.

The house was absolutely fantastic. It would have cost at least a half a million dollars to have the quality of a house like that built anywhere in the United States not counting the price of the property.

There was custom handlaid

Above, Middle Left and Below: A man examines the damage done to his home by a bomb attack. The man who was highly educated in the old regime quickly made himself available to the coalition forces as an interpreter in downtown Baghdad. The anti-Iraqi insurgents found him out and attacked his home while he was at work. The man's wife was at home asleep next to the exterior wall when an insurgent threw the bomb over the fence and it detonated about two feet outside from where she was sleeping. When the bomb detonated, it blew a small crater in the ground and blew out all the windows on the same side of the house and all the windows in the neighboring houses for 70 meters in all directions. The wife awoken and alarmed, called her husband while he was in a high level meeting with LTC Welch and told him what had happened. Both men raced out of the meeting and LTC Welch went to his Personal Security Detachment (PSD) and insisted on hurrying to southwestern Baghdad in the Al Mansoor district to show a sign of support and a give a presence to the situation. We arrived and patrolled the ground on foot to clear any possible secondary explosive devices. The man invited LTC Welch in to examine the damage, who in turn quickly invited me in to document the event with my camera. I was amazed at what I saw. The quality of the house alone would have cost $500,000 anywhere in the US. I was absolutely amazed by the Arab hospitality as the women who had been just a few feet from a good size explosion scurried around fixing iced colas for the guests and insisted on waiting on us.

stone work throughout the entire house. It was about a 3-4000 sqft home with 12-foot ceilings. The whole house had reinforced concrete with small windows. It was absolutely amazing. The man showed us throughout the whole house.

I photographed all the broken glass and such. The bomb blew out the windows on one side of the house and all the windows across the street, but it did not break through the exterior wall.

The woman of the house was sleeping on the inside of the wall that was blown up and she was not harmed at all. The crater left by the bomb was about 2.5 feet diameter and about 8 inches deep.

The thing that was most

The wealthier neighborhoods of western Baghdad from the air in a Blackhawk.

amazing to me was the fact that an Arab woman had almost lost her life. Her brother had just been killed that week, she had two foreign soldiers walking around in her home with weapons and, God forbid, their boots on in an Islamic home, and all she could do was scurry around fixing fancy glasses of ice and pepsi on a silver tray to treat the guests with hospitality. I just couldn't believe it. The police finally showed up and she treated them with the same hospitality.

We left and came back to post. I was supposed to go out patrolling that night but I had to cancel because I was walking crooked from being so tired after the long day, a lot of which was out in the sun. The next day I slept forever because I was so exhausted.

My first day on the day shift was surprisingly slow, but picked up towards the end when I had to pick up a journalist from the San Francisco Chronicle named John Koopman. I spent a couple of hours arranging his convoy to the marines to the west of us over in Falluja. I took him over to the Air Force's terminal which looks just like a scene out of an old MASH episode. We smoked some good cigars together

and I counted my first day on the day shift a huge blessing. John sure seemed like a real good person.

Two days later I got a call to go down to the International Zone (Green Zone) in central Baghdad for a civil affairs conference. It was really amazing. I learned all the details about the status of the infrastructure. I found it really interesting. I want to write an article on it and I might, but right now I am writing you all this e-mail, which like everything else

An up-armored Humvee drives over a Bailey Bridge that was erected by engineers to cover up the massive hole in the concrete bridge left by what was probably a dump truck bearing IED. Towards the end of our tour this became a standard practice for taking out bridges and slowing down growth of the infrastructure.

that I write, has turned out to be much more than originally intended.

When I got back John Koopman was there at the building. Evidently the marines don't want anymore press in Falluja so he decided to stay. He was pretty upset about it. I invited him to go to the Burger King here with me and we had dinner and then a good cigar together. This is the end of the second day on the day shift and it was just incredible.

A final note. I have been having serious trouble with foot rot the past two or three

months. I finally got it cured by changing to cotton socks. Miraculous.

_____

August 03, 2004

I was able to take a day off from work and for the very first time it was during the day when all the shops were open. It was great, I really enjoyed it. With all the headaches of the day shift, it is still better than the night shift as I found out. This was probably my first enjoyable day off since I got here. I went and had a massive workout over in South

A common sight in Baghdad near the end of OIF II was throngs of men lined up to sign up for something. There was no telling what they were waiting for in this line.

Victory's gym. Then I went swimming in Ude Hussein's private pool in the lake. There are little islands in the man made lake that you have all seen pictures of. On one of the islands there are two tower type apartments and in between them there is a really beautiful pool. I went swimming all by myself. I was surrounded by all the palaces and the aquamarine water of the lake. It was pure heaven for an hour. Later I went shopping and bought a bunch of polished bronze trinkets and one large brass piece to add to my collection. I also bought a Huca. That looks like a Turkish bong, but I smoke tobacco out of it, not hashish. It's more work than smoking a regular pipe.

One of the great thrills for me during the year long tour was to climb TELECOM Tower near downtown Baghdad at night. The lights were wonderful and misleading. Most of the lights in western Baghdad were from privately owned generators owned by wealthy people who had prospered under Saddam Hussein.

August 03, 2004

There is a lot of go-home-itus going on here and I'm really starting to feel it. We are now about five and a half months along here in theater and just about to the hump day three weeks into this month. We all have our noses pointed towards the barn already, but we're not there yet.

It's interesting how we all seem to go through similar psychological phases as we all progress through this tour of duty. In some ways we're all getting along better and in some ways we're not. There is always the underlying "I don't have things exactly the way I want" frustration here. I am doing everything I can do to fight it and then encourage those around me to accept that which we cannot change, and I really need to start standing up and change the things that I can.

I have reached a milestone here. I am now completely debt free. I have paid off the last of my student loans. It is a good feeling. I am taking over the office boy work from a colleague who is going home on leave. To tell you the truth I am thinking about going to Europe on my leave. I want to go home, but I also want to take advantage of the free round-trip ticket to Europe. Don't know what I will do once I am there, but I'll probably ride the trains and drink beer. Sounds like a plan to me.

I bought a bicycle and can now get around a little better. Soon the weight rooms will be done and I'll be able to get to working out more. That will be a welcome facility. It has taken forever for the army to get a decent weight room built here. They built one but decided that the cheap construction was a fire hazard right after they finished it and closed it down. The army then started rebuilding another structure, but this time it's the second cheapest form

Captain Tim Tate poses at the restaurant level of TELECOM Tower where Saddam Hussein and his family were the only people reported by locals to have been allowed to dine there. A more likely scenario would have been that the restaurant was reserved only for high ranking Ba'ath party members.

I took this photo from inside the back of a fast moving Humvee and it wasn't until later when I downloaded the photos onto the computer that I noticed the outdoor flower shop in the background. This photo became my greatest evidence that our year in Baghdad was not in vain. This flower shop represented not only the entire infrastructure that it took to grow, harvest, transport and to put them into colorful pots, but also the people who had the where-with-all to buy such frivolous gifts for special occasions to justify the existence of such a shop. It is very ironic, but it took a flower shop to show me that our year was not in vain. We mattered. We knew that this year of our life was our greatest contribution to the world.

very aggressively and forcefully, because that is what the Iraqi people really respect.

August 15, 2004

There isn't much new to report on today. This was one of the better days I've had here in Baghdad. If they were all like this, then I would want to stay. I started out going to church this morning and it's a really great service, very lively. I was very inspired. After that I was told to take it easy today, because this past week was so hectic. So I took it easy and smoked a big cigar instead of a small cigar. I am now completely acclimated to the heat because I can enjoy a good cigar out in the heat no matter how warm it gets out there.

John Koopman from the San Francisco Chronicle wrote some good articles about us. It's amazing how

of construction.

August 08, 2004

There has been so much going on and I have been so busy that I haven't been able to write to you all. I have been working with some notable people in the press. I have a picture coming up with me and Martha Raddatz from ABC News. I keep trying to get the press to cover all the projects that we're doing over here and they all say the same thing, "We want to get our stories out there and nobody cares about sewers and electricity." The headquarters for these places only want the doom and gloom and nothing else. I am trying to get the news out to you guys.

There really isn't much to the recent uprising or

fighting that you're hearing about. It is so much smaller than the April rebellion you wouldn't believe it, but it is something. I can't say much about it because I am exposed to all the classified stuff, but I will tell you this, the Iraqi security forces are doing a much better job than before. The Iraqis will soon be able to take some real control over their own security. Soon being six months to a year in my opinion.

The commanding general ordered an impromptu press conference late last night and we all stayed up late last night trying to arrange for that to happen. This morning was a madhouse getting it all together. I had a major role in getting the western media there. When you see General Chiarelli on TV, you will know that I had a lot to do with it. He was speaking

Above: A busy market street thriving with business, mainly produce, was another common sight in Baghdad. Below: A typical street in downtown Baghdad with congestion.

49

you can tell the professionals from the wannabees. This guy just acted like a pro and he got the stories he wanted and some he wasn't counting on in a short amount of time. Everyone liked him. It was great to sit and visit with him over a good cigar.

Life is fun in the fast lane here. I can't wait for the weight room to open up. Tomorrow is supposed to be my day off. We'll see if it comes to pass.

August 27, 2004
Great Cigar Moment by the Lake with a GUY

It's been a while since I have written you all, I know, but that is one of the joys of working the day shift on a skeleton crew. The time has been flying by, but I haven't had time to write a lot and I haven't gone outside the wire at all so there aren't any pictures. The month of August has gone by in a blink and I'm glad about that.

I have my vacation time now as September 17th through October 8th. I'll be going to Edinburgh Scotland, Dublin Ireland and Bremen Germany. I'll be staying at a one fancy hotel in Edinburgh and then in a small one in Dublin near the Guinness Brewery. Yes I'm going to the holy lands. Bremen is where I was stationed many years ago and I might be able to stay with friends there. It will be Octobefest in Bremen when I get there. Darn the bad timing: the crowds, the prices, hotel rooms non-available. What will I do?

I escorted a reporter from the Associated Press. He interviewed the commanding general MG Chiarelli for Time Magazine and then we had time to kill. It was one of the better cigar moments

One of my final media escort missions was to transport Shepherd Smith (on the right side) from Fox News, from the Air Pax Terminal to a hotel near the Baghdad International Airport.

I've had. The sunset, the lake, and a guy. Why is it always a guy Lord? I turned to him and asked him why he couldn't be one of those tiny little hotty correspondents. He replied that he was thinking the same thing about me.

The day after that I escorted John Burns of the New York Times, who has also been doing work as a correspondent for CNN lately. I escorted media all day long. I loved it, but I was exhausted at the end.

The other captain is back and now the social dynamics have gotten interesting. I have been working with the Iraqi media and employees and trying to get every-

Jim Krane of Associated Press was one of the very best reporters I had the privilege of dealing with. Here he is smoking one of my cigars. This man sat on our porch and typed out a simple story about what was going on in Baghdad that day, hooked his laptop up to the satellite phone, pushed the send button and continued to puff on one of my cigars. An hour later I went into the office and did a news search to see what the media was saying about us that day and there was his story on many newspapers from around the world.

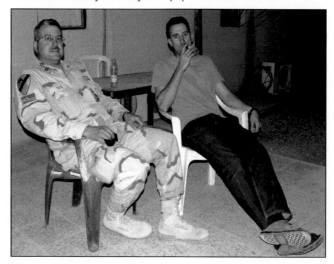

thing under contract. It's a real mess. I'm praying for success more than trying to work for completion of this task. The whole Iraqi system is so corrupt and now I am knee deep into it.

August 24, 2004

We have been putting out a bi-monthly newspaper and in the last issue there was an article about the homosexual poet's park. There is a huge park in downtown Baghdad called Abu Nuwas, that is much larger than Central Park in New York and much more a part of the local culture. The general took on this park, which is the cultural icon for not only Baghdad, but also for all of Iraq, as his own pet project. As we did the initial research we became aware of what Mr. Nuwas was so happy about, and we all sat around and wondered who was going to tell the general that his pet project was named after a man who liked little boys and really enjoyed telling the whole world about it. I was laughing hysterically. The general finally found out about it. Take note of this park and the name, because Abu Nuwas is to Baghdad, what Central Park, all the parks with monuments in DC and the Champ Laisse' in Paris are to all those cities. It's huge and a very large part of the culture revolves around it. You should be so glad to be enlightened by me.

August 29, 2004

The mood here is tense as people begin to realize that eventually we'll reach a point where things continuously slow down and there probably won't be future major rebellions like we have seen in the past. That means people are starting to wonder what they are going to be doing around the office when the media doesn't care about 1st Cavalry Division anymore.

You all know that whenever you have a lot of government employees with too little to do, the politics can get ugly. That's what I am expecting this situation to come to. The good thing is that will be an excellent tell-tale sign that we have really won the war and that it will be all progress from here on out.

I have found more religious functions and people to talk to which is always good. The main chaplain is back from leave now and it was good to see him again.

Speaking of leave, I am really looking forward to going to Europe now. I was kind of dreading this up coming vacation.

Here are some of the main thoughts that soldiers are facing on taking leave. Going home is great and painful. It heals the relationships and hurts the kids all over again. Saying goodbye the second time around after

John Koopman from the San Francisco Chronicle was a real good guy. We smoked a couple of my cigars together while we waited for the aircraft to come and pick him up. We were frustrated with the media's cold shoulder towards all the positives that were going on. We asked John, like everyone else, to go on a tour of infrastructure projects that were finally coming to completion. His stay was extended unexpectedly and he went out on the tour and then reported on what he saw and a very rare article appeared in the San Francisco Chronicle about what we were doing over here in between all the bad news. All we were asking for was some fair reporting.

only two weeks being back is much worse then when you said goodbye the first time.

It is clearly worth it for a family man to go home on leave and it is clearly not worth it for a single soldier to go home on leave. Some who can afford it are having the kids stay with Grandma and Grandpa and the spouse is flying out to link up in Frankfurt.

Even fewer are asking not to take leave at all because of the foreseen problems. Those are pretty much the options that soldiers are facing.

———————————

August 31, 2004

Things have been pretty busy around here lately. I have been moving reporters around and trying to entertain them as much as possible. I haven't been able to sleep well over the past couple of nights and I'm just a zombie today. I hate that feeling.

My cigar smoking buddy has been promising a Cougar flag signed sealed and delivered

in a a few weeks. Well Keith Bloom, who is somewhere high up on the who's who at WSU, bought a flag and took it around and got athletes to sign it, to include the head coach of the football team, Bill Doba. Keith sent out some pictures of the volleyball team holding the flag up. I can't wait for it to get here. Hey Keith buddy, can you cancel the flag and send the volleyball team. Just kidding... NOT.

The crew from 60 Minutes is in the area and everyone is on pins and needles waiting to see what kind of stunts they pull. We have really been hit with some real winners lately.

We seem to get the real interesting reporters whenever the action heats up. Not to say it's all thier fault. Every time the action heats up all the officers and soldiers get hardly any sleep and then they get grouchy and that's when all the fun begins.

I am trying to work around both and get my job accomplished. I was telling someone yesterday that it was real fun escorting the reporters around and answering telephones, all you have to do is learn to smile and enjoy being lied to. Too easy.

There is this one reporter that I swear, every time he calls me on my cell phone, I feel like I need to wipe off the phone with toilet paper because he is just so full of it.

I could whine and moan, rant and rave all day, but I need to get back to slacking off.

Martha Raddatz from ABC Nightline was one of the first celebrities that I had the opportunity to escort. She liked my cigar.

John Burns became a celebrity in Baghdad as he dabbled in correspondent work with CNN. He is a journalist with the New York Times.

September 06, 2004

The weather is cooling off now. The daily highs are around 105 to 108 now. Soon it will be down to the 100s. The problem is that when it gets that low, the humidity skyrockets up making for an incredibly hot and muggy experience.

I am hoping to miss the hot and muggy transition with the 20 day leave I am taking to Europe. By the time I get back in early October, it should be the beginning of the autumn rainy season and I will only have 4.5 months left. That's if I don't get extended. If I were extended six months, I wouldn't complain a bit. I believe in what I am doing.

I had a really nice visit with a southern belle from the Arkansas Newspaper here covering the Arkansas National Guard. I took her out to my favorite cigar smoking spot that is soooo romantic that I wrote you about last time where I am always with a guy. We watched the sunset together and for the first time I was finally with a woman and you know what I did... I smoked a cigar while she jibber-jabbared away the whole time. It was a real nice visit, but I won't be complaining about smoking cigars at sunset with other guys anymore.

I read in the Newspaper that we captured the King of Clubs the other day and killed off 70 of his immediate followers while capturing another 80. That is one of the bigger captures in a very long time. Things are definitely looking up around here. We are having another windfall of success here lately at getting many of the bad guys.

The progress is steadily chugging along and I think that

there will be a huge explosion of progress here in a little bit after we get a few obstacles out of the way, one of those

The best college football watching buddy anybody ever had, bought this flag and used his contacts to get into the athletic department to get the signatures of all the athletes and coaches along with the town mayor and Butch T. Coug. He sent it out to me and it was the best gift anyone ever gave me. It will forever be one of my most favorite sports mementos. I took the flag around and found other soldiers from the state of Washington who were fellow Coug fans and had my pictures taken with them. The flag encouraged many of us over there in Iraq. See Sept 28 entry.

being electricity 24/7 and the other being security.

It will be amazing how

things change over the next six months in Baghdad. The wheels of industry are starting to grind a little bit here in

western Baghdad and soon there will be a better sense of what freedom and democ-

racy are really all about in the minds of many Iraqis.

You should always remember that these people don't know what it is to have freedom. They really had no clue as to what we were and what we still are really trying to accomplish here. Now thanks to the efforts of the Iraqi media, they are starting to realize that we are here to bring them democracy, stability and a functional sewage infrastructure. That's a good definition of freedom if ever I heard one.

Lately I have been working on the writing of contract proposals for the Iraqi media director, advisor and translators that we've been using to help get the Iraqi press agencies to cover our work and progress. This is the only way to get the message out to the Iraqi people and it is working. I thank God for the opportunity to serve in this capacity, because I earnestly believe that facilitating the Arab media is the single most important thing that I will do in the fight for Baghdad and the fight against terrorism.

The articles written in the local papers are making it all the way around the Arab region. I prayed for the opportunity to help out with the Arab media while I was on night shift and now I am knee deep in it. I will be arranging, organizing and reporting the Arab media coverage of 1st Cavalry Division media events, arranging the Arab media coming onto post and going outside the wire and bringing them in through the inspections and gates. Be careful for what you pray for.

A huge boost in my own morale was when soldiers reported killing many enemy insurgents during the last uprising in Sadr City, and when they came back the next day, the bodies were still there. This was the first time that the Arabs left the bodies out overnight.

The significance of this is that the Koran teaches that when a person dies, their remains must be buried before sunset or else they go to hell and remain there until somebody properly buries the corpse. The people have turned against the Mehdi militia that they are purposely leaving their remains out to rot signifying that they want these people to burn in hell. Three days after the major fire fight, the Iraqi Government had to arrange to have the bodies dealt with.

One person postulated that the dead insurgents could have been foreigners come here to fight the Americans, while another reasoned, that we killed so many of the bad guys that there is not enough left to bury their own dead. Since this was the first time that we saw this, it stands to reason to me that the local community has been thoroughly turned against the insurgents and I believe this is from getting the information out on the progress we're striving for through the local Iraqi media.

Needless to say, I am very biased on the importance of getting the Iraqi media to cover the military's efforts because what we're doing is a good thing and any reporting on this will make us look good in the local community.

Another possible success here for me personally is that media director Ude that we hired and I am now writing the contract proposal for, saved enough money, bought a printing press and started his own weekly paper. He made contacts with so many Baghdad newspaper reporters at the conferences he helped coordinate for us, that he was able to hire many of

them away from their newspapers. Every one of his weekly papers has a page dedicated to the 1st Cavalry Division's

Top: an unknown Cougar fan on the left and Sergeant Milun on the right. Middle: football team signatures.
Below: girls soccer and volleyball team signatures.

The Cougar football team along with some coaches and the town mayor, Glen Johnson, who is also the voice of the Cougs at most sporting events, signed the flag in support of troops deployed overseas.

efforts in the Baghdad area. I hope that this paper is a success and takes off. Ude wants to make it a daily paper as

soon as possible.

Another thing that I am doing is escorting the western media around here on the

installation as you have seen in the pictures. Things have slowed down and are getting slower. We have all been

bored here as of late. I hope things will pick up, after I leave for Europe.

Well I have written way too much and interjected my opinions again like I said I wouldn't do any more. However, one of my predictions on the possible alliances between the three major factions is starting to come about, according to one local Iraqi.

If you remember, for those few of you who read it, I predicted in the advent of failure in our attempt to stabilize the country and impute a democratic form of government, two of the three factions would unite leaving the third in a defensive posture.

The Iraqi I talked to said that it is now being seen or feared to be happening, but more with voting for the future Prime Minister than with an organized rebellion.

The other problem is that it is the union of Kurds with Sunni to thwart the all out domination at the ballot box for the much more populated Shiites in southern Iraq.

This was the one union I predicted would never happen and we absolutely didn't need to worry about. Not only did I write absolutely horribly, but I predicted the wrong thing. To my credit, at least I was looking at possible alliances between the ethnicities. Nobody else that I talked to here has been thinking along those lines. I get an E for effort.

I always said, "Be humble or be humbled." Now I are humbled.

September 12, 2004

So much is happening lately that I haven't had time to write you all. I was able to get outside the wire and I'm fine, so now I can write about it. I now have many pictures to show everyone.

I embedded with three different Artillery Batteries (companies of about 75 soldiers) and went out on patrols with them. It was the most fantastic experience so far I think. The artillerymen, who are said to be the soldiers who never walk because their cannons were the one weapon that was way to heavy to carry, are now the only one's in Baghdad that patrol on foot.

These soldiers from the 3rd Battalion, 82nd Field Artillery Regiment patrol near the International Zone in downtown Baghdad and the area is very stable and probably the safest area of Baghdad. I will be describing my experience with them over the next handful of e-mails.

For this e-mail I am going to talk about the army's "mother of all toolboxes." I know that there are many on the distro-list out there who are manly men with manly shops and manly tool boxes. Well you're going to love these photographs of the army's new toolbox/garage/ crane. The army didn't fool around. They came up with a 5 ton toolbox with a 10 ton crane attached to it.

The whole box is pulled up onto the back of a 20 ton cargo hauling truck. The crew drives to the area of repair and slides the tool box

An artilleryman carries out last minute preparation for the upcoming patrol at night in downtown Baghdad as the sun goes down.

off the back of the truck and then they go to work and lift the engine out using the crane attached to the side and set up to do machine work as well. The reason the toolbox is not permanently on the back of the truck is it is more convenient to haul it somewhere, off load it, and then drive the truck away to

haul something else. I don't think I saw an air conditioner in the box, but it has everything else.

To Kevin, Gary, Larry and Dad; see, there are tools out there that you guys don't have yet.

___

September 28, 2004

I fully intend to embarrass Keith Bloom with gratitude for his gift. He bought a Cougar flag and took it around to all the athletes for signatures.

Many people have been encouraged by the show of support, not only by Keith for doing this, but also for the athletes who signed it.

Way to go Keith. Thanks from Baghdad. Thanks to any of the student athletes and the local city and school

leaders that showed their support as well.

Go Cougs.

___

October 24, 2004

The saddest story in Baghdad: In the early hours one morning, in the hottest time of the summer a patrol was called on the radio to stop a large truck with people throwing bombs out the back in Sadr City. They fired the vehicle up and it caught fire.

They rushed to the scene and secured the area. There were many bodies on the ground and some screaming and some with minor injuries.

One man was clearly about to die and was screaming in a great deal of pain. The sergeant went to the lieutenant and asked permission to put the man out of his misery. The LT gave him the go ahead.

The sergeant ordered a private to do it but he refused to do so, so the sergeant tried to kill him with a machinegun that jammed. Seeing this, another sergeant grabbed a smaller machinegun and shot the body with a burst of bullets. He walked away, but the man continued to move so the first sergeant, finally with the machinegun cleared and ready, shot him one more time killing the individual.

The platoon was in horror with what they saw. When they returned, the company commander didn't even have to ask if something happened. He separated everyone from each other and began to ask questions and thus started a long investigation.

The sergeants have both been charged with murder, because there is no such thing as mercy killing, not even in battle. The lieuten-

A mansion in western Baghdad from the old regime.

The soldiers from the 3-82 Field Artillery Regiment after having the medals pinned on them by the Battery Commander, Lieutenant Colonel Vuono (seen below) Front row left to right: SGT Lucero, SGT Bier, SPC Tower, Unknown, Unknown. Back Row: SGT Pilgrim, SGT Arthur, SGT Berntain, SPC Sesters, Unknown, SSG McMurray.

Iraqi people.

There are five soldiers from the same platoon charged with murder and conspiracy to commit murder and other related charges. The murders didn't even occur in the same month.

This is an excellent example of really poor leadership with some determined hard headed jerks underneath bound and determined to play by their own rules.

They should make a mocumentary movie out of this one platoon to show incoming lieutenants what will happen to them if they don't take responsibility and wield their authority wisely.

Looking forward to getting back now.

November 01, 2004

It's raining, its raining, its raining. We finally reached the winter season. God bless

Lieutenant Colonel Vouno commander of the 3rd Battery of the 82nd Field Artillery Regiment talks to his troops at the awards ceremony.

ant, who is under investigation and will probably be charged with conspiracy to murder, was called to testify and with eyes filled with tears and skin white as a ghost, he pleaded the 5th amendment.

The sergeants were described as "go to sergeants" with great potential in the army. If convicted, and I think they will be convicted of something, they will be sentenced to a minimum of life in prison.

Two good sergeants spending the rest of their lives in prison for putting an Iraqi out of his misery when they were certain that he was going to die anyway.

I wondered what the lieutenant was going through, I wondered if he was a fellow brother in the Lord, but mostly I just felt sick to my stomach for all of them.

Today when I was leaving the chapel service I saw the lieutenant. He was there in the chapel service. I don't

know if he came because he is at a rock bottom point in his life, I don't know if he came because he is a solid believer, but he came. All I can do is pray for him either way.

There are always two sides to the story on these matters. Some of the testimonies say the screaming man wasn't in such bad shape. Many of the soldiers in the platoon called it murder. Some leaders have said that they expected problems like this from many of the soldiers in this unit, because it is their second tour in Iraq and many of them were on the invading force with 3rd Infantry Division. Maybe we'll see more of this as many more soldiers are brought into Iraqi Freedom III that were part of the invasion force.

These moral dilemmas in the gray area of right and wrong have me sick to my stomach. You have got to pray and fight to avoid these scenarios.

(Taken from December 06, 2004) Today I started escort-

ing media to the hearings for soldiers who are charged with murdering unarmed the army because now that we are done with the high temperatures of spring summer and fall, we just now have received air conditioning in our Humvees. After being here for eight months and only having three months to go. Two of our four Humvees now have the armor add on kits for our protection. God bless the army for preparing us for war now that our tour of duty is almost over. Gotta love the army.

Today is kind of crazy. The one-star general is being interviewed by TV. The TV crews were late because of traffic downtown. The frequency jammers at the gates keep us from communicating with cell phones which makes the colonels and majors explode with anxiety over the "unknown". There is so much going on now, but I can't describe half of it. I'll e-mail you all later to let you know the latest twists and turns in life.

a mile away. The attack took place out on the main highway to the airport where there are many inspectors, mostly Nepalese conducting inspection of

Above and Below: Purple Hearts and Army Commendation Medals await being pinned on the well deserving soldiers of the 3-82 Artillery Regiment.

am absolutely exhausted. Just droning through the day. Hoping to get my haircut tonight. The weather has let up some and the

vehicles going to the airport. This tragic event rocked everybody's world today. No American soldiers were killed, but it closed down all the gates and stopped people from coming on and off the base.

I worked out last night and then couldn't sleep at all. I

mud is starting to dry up. Maybe I hadn't mentioned it, but the rains hit and the whole place turned to a mud pit.

I think that people's attitudes have really gone down around here. People are all looking a bit down

and I myself am on a bit of a rocky road, or perhaps I should say I'm mired down on the muddy road.

We have hit the final quarter and have probably just under 100 days left in Baghdad. The main bulk of 1st CAV Division has about 120 days left. We are all nearing the end, but it isn't there yet.

There is this psychological phase I think that we can smell the fresh air coming through the end of the tunnel, but we can't see the light at the end of the tunnel yet. That combined with the mud and muck is probably causing the doldrums a bit.

November 04, 2004

The sun has come out and the mud is drying up and the elections are finally over and the spirits are lifting, to include mine. Yes I put out the whine and the gripe that things were gloomy over here, and many of you responded well with prayer and concern and e-mails that bolstered my spirit.

Other factors were the increase in defense security in anticipation of the looming US elections had us running around in the Kevlar and frag vests even to go to the bathroom. Now that the elections are over, we were able to take them off and it's back to uniform and soft cap.

Many were worried about the elections and as you can

November 03, 2004

We had a VBIED hit close to home today. I was just entering the plastic out-house when I heard the ear shattering blast that was a little over

Major General Chiarelli ordered his staff officers to go out on patrol with the soldiers in regular patrolling units. This directive was intended for the lieutenant colonels and majors that worked for him at the division main headquarters, but they almost always delegated it down to subordinate officers like myself who gladly jumped at the opportunity. I had the privilege of going with the 3rd Battalion of 82nd Field Artillery for three days. These artilleryman go out in up-armored Humvees and then dismount to patrol the streets of western Baghdad both during the day and at night. The above photo is of a platoon conducting a foot patrol near the Um al Tabul Mosque in downtown Baghdad. The soldiers often go to these outdoor gyros cafes to check on the owners and make sure that nobody is threatening them or trying to harass them, and oh-by-the-way, order a really good kabob right off the grill while they're there.

imagine, the military tends to favor Bush a little bit so there is renewed optimism.

Receiving e-mails telling me about invites to dinner, stogies and a few rounds down at the bar have given me renewed optimistic out-

look for my return home.

All these reasons have culminated in my renewed invigorated attitude. I FEEL JUST SPIFFY.

———————————

November 08, 2004

One of the main goals for foot patrols in Baghdad was to talk with the local people and simply ask them questions about what was going on. Above: The interpreter asks some local men visiting in the cooler midnight temperatures if they knew where any bad guys were. Left: The soldiers ask young men what they were doing out at midnight.

The boss is back from leave and I must admit I am glad he is here. He has been able to encourage me. I received a "well done good and faithful deputy director" from him as he has been monitoring my work via the Internet. He just gave me a pep talk and hopefully he will be able to keep me on as his assistant, otherwise it's back to the night shift. Right now I don't care what I do, I just want to have an effective part in the overall war over here and I believe as he does that what we are doing in getting the local Iraqi media to cover the military and what we're doing over here is a very important piece of the puzzle.

They are sending out the warnings to soldiers for the upcoming holidays. If soldiers receive multiple shipments of alcohol from various sources they are being prosecuted. The military is dead serious. Many of you have expressed an interest in sending a Christmas package or such. Please don't send alcohol.

I plan on getting into the Christmas spirit this year by sending gifts to many of you. So... to anyone who has sent me something through the year. I need to make sure

A Humvee moves out into the darkness after soldiers dropped off boxes of clothes that had been sent by a family member from home. Many boxes of children clothes were liberated from attics all over America and went to the welcoming arms of many Iraqi families.

that I have a current mailing address. Do not play the "I don't want a soldier sending me anything" because this is more for me than it is for you. I have to go through "retail therapy" and "gift wrapping" therapy to be a part of the holiday season this year, because it is the only thing I can do.

_____

A Humvee from the 3-82 Field Artillery moves out in downtown Baghdad. These patrols were crucial to the success in finding insurgents and establishing relations with the average Iraqi.

November 17, 2004

What's wrong with Hara?

Most soldiers coming back will be forever changed by their experience here in Iraq and I am sure I will be one of them. I am certain that many positive changes have been taking place in my life as I have been exposed to many experiences while living in a fairly safe environment.

It is obvious that every Iraqi's life has been forever changed by our presence here. Today I want to share a story with you all that I have come across about how both a lieutenant colonel (LTC) and a young girl have changed each others lives forever.

LTC Richard Welch is the Division Civil Affairs Officer who travels around Baghdad meeting with mid to high ranking formal and informal societal leaders here. He is a reservist and is actually a county district attorney in the state of Ohio.

While walking back and forth between meetings in

one building downtown Baghdad, he kept seeing injured people in a line outside an office for civilian claims against the military. In this line there was a little girl in great pain. He walked by her twice and then the third time he had to stop and find out what her story was.

Her name is Hara. Hara had been playing with her sister nearly a year ago, before 1st Cavalry Division arrived in Baghdad. An IED explosion killed her sister and severely burned her legs. The burnt tissue scabbed up in such a way that it contracted, leaving her legs bent and unable to straighten. She had not walked since the day she sustained the injuries.

Her mother is a neglected second wife who now receives little attention or support from her husband. Not only this, but it's her job to raise her children and the children of the new wife in the ghettos of southern Baghdad.

She had been trying to get her daughter medical

attention and make a claim against the US to receive money. The mother had been trying in futility for about eight months when LTC Welch found her that day. He saw her blackened and scabbed legs that had open fissures that were badly infected and seeping fluid.

Enough was enough. He investigated enough to find out that Hara's claim had been lost. He insisted on taking her to American medics for attention. They treated her wounds. She and her mother were taken back to their house in the slums. Some time ago she was taken to a normal hospital and had some very bad experiences there.

She was taken back home where a man came to their house claiming to be a doctor from their tribe. He insisted that he could heal her and there was no need for Americans to help out anyone from their tribe. The man took a straight razor and slit the scar tissue behind each knee and then slammed down on her knees with all his might. The legs had not been straightened in 10 months. The man had dislocated both knees and broke one of the tibia bones in her right leg.

LTC Welch came to check on her and found out what had been happening to Hara and was outraged. Colonels who are outraged tend to get their way. He had his soldier take her to the American hospital at one of the major bases in southern Baghdad and insisted they treat her and put her up there. She had been there for a week and everyone fell in love with her and many cried the day we came to pick her up.

I was traveling with the security detachment the day they transported her from the American army clinic to a specialty hospital in central

Above: The December trip around Baghdad necessitated soldiers to bundle up. People familiar with the Humvees used for these missions can recognize the red dot air-conditioning that was finally installed on the Shadow Force's vehicles after the blistering high temperatures of summer were finally over. Below: As the convoy turned the corner we immediately saw a man on the roof with a sniper rifle. Should I shoot or should I shoot (camera) flashed through my mind. The kevelar helmet tipped me off and he wasn't pointing the rifle at us made me realize that this was probably a friendly Iraqi sniper. I asked SSG Gray how he knew that this was a friendly. He replied that he didn't. The helmet tipped him off as well. This neighborhood was just outside of Sadr City where many neighborhood watches had put snipers on rooftops for necessary security. The rifle used is probably the Russian Dragunov.

Baghdad that LTC Welch had researched out himself. The hospital was Hussein's private hospital that had been fully modernized and equipped.

The day started with us going to the mother's house in the slums. It was quite the eye-opener as I was standing up by the machinegunner as we traveled so I could get better pictures and more of them. Recent rains had left small ponds everywhere in the entire Baghdad area and these ponds serve as instant sewer ponds and stank horribly. The convoy traveled down ever narrowing roads and alleyways until we were pinched in between the concrete houses where Hara lived. I was invited in to the simple house where I was allowed to take pictures and then we sat down as Hara's older sister insisted we have chai tea and morning bread with them. She waited on us. The 15 year old was giddy and uncontrollably excited to have American soldiers in her house. She was full of hormones and falling in love with every man that came through the door. It was truly an amazing thing to see all this.

Meanwhile outside the soldiers stood guard and kids from the neighborhood swarmed all over the soldiers and Humvees crying out for attention. The mother decided that she could not go with us so we left.

We entered the army hospital and I met Hara. Diana, an Arab American from San Diego working with the army as a translator, served as surrogate mother. She got involved with the "Hara Project" from early on and lived for each possible visit.

The doctor, Dianna and the colonel took turns carrying Hara out to the Humvee as she received many hugs and kisses from the staff. We drove through town to the new hospi-

This crowded market place was a dangerous location to become canalized as we found out. We soon became engulfed in bumper to bumper stop and go traffic making for a nervous and tense situation as seen in the pictures below.

tal near Haifa Street.

We went into the building and I was amazed that there were working lights, elevators and escalators. We took her up to the 10th floor to a room with men between 25 and 35 who all had injuries associated with war wounds. The colonel did not want a 13 year old girl staying in a room with men who quite likely were terrorists, especially when she was being brought there by US soldiers.

Colonels tend to get their way and she was taken to a room down the hall where she was all by herself. This is where I took the parting shots and then took some scenic photos out the windows of Baghdad.

LTC Welch's parting comments to me struck me hard. "I can only hope for the day that I can see her walk and run like a normal child." The comment struck me and I could not forget it. The day that Hara stands up and walks like a normal person will be the day that LTC Welch is exonerated, and his efforts will not have been in vain.

I continued to dwell on this entire event and the meaning of this young girl who has been through such trauma that she should have every right to want death to end it all, but has survived and still has the chance to struggle to eventually "rise up and walk." I learned some difficult things that day.

I left on a convoy that morning with the desire to get outside the wire and I came back a different person. LTC Welch is going to be a different person when he gets back, and it's obvious that Hara will be forever changed.

(Taken from November 27, 2004) Many asked about the pictures in the background inside Hara's home. Those are Imams. You see Muhammad had a bunch of daugh-

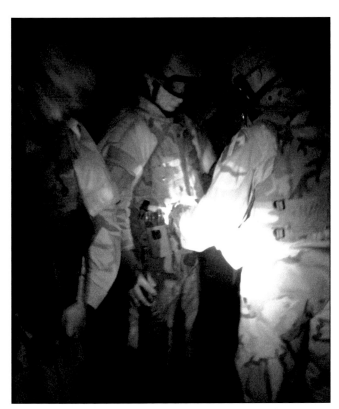

Above and Right: A Sergeant performs last minute Pre-Combat Checks and Inspections in the dark prior to leaving on the mission.

ters and he married them off to influential men who became Imams or clergymen that followed after his teaching and evidently there was a lineage of 12 Imams that are considered to be prophets after Muhammad.

The Shiites believe that these 12 Imams were prophets and follow after their teaching and the Sunni and Kurds do not. People will identify with one of the Imams over the others for one reason or another and carry their picture with them in their cars or put pictures up in their houses.

November 21, 2004

See!!! It was a great year after all. Yes I must gloat just a little bit about the Cougs.

The generals all want to get their stories and their messages out to the Iraqi people and I organize and facilitate the Iraqi media to show up and get them through all the security and check points

and then bring them in.

I have to tell you the story of the backdrop. We have this background of blue with the US and Iraqi flag on it and we have all the interviews take place in front of this backdrop. It is something we put together one night before a major press conference. The blue material in the background consists of common sheets that we bought at the PX for $5 and the flags were on sale for a buck each so the generals stage cost one of our sergeants $7 total. The generals love it and it looks great on TV. Many press members have had their picture taken in front of the now well known "1st CAV Studio" because they want to prove that they have been in such a famous place.

November 26, 2004

The weather has clearly turned to cold and now the nights are down into the thirties. I will share with you a

true story about the military life so you good voting tax paying citizens can have a small clue as to what military BS is all about.

When we began to deploy less than a year from the elections, any politician voting against a bill that gave our soldiers better equipment would have committed political suicide. All of a sudden there was money for everything. The taxpayers, uh I mean the voters, wanted to know that the American troops had every convenience, so instead of drawing wool long johns and old down sleeping bags, we had the latest state of the art light weight, high-speed camping gear in tan, green and black colors. It was great. It was like we just robbed an REI

outlet store.

One of the delightful new commodities that the taxpayers, uh I mean soon to be voters, had purchased with all of your hard borrowed money was a very nice black fleece pull over, of the $150 price range compared to similar quality at an REI store. Needless to say that those fleece pullovers have never been in the military inventory and there is no place for them in the regulations for uniform (AR 670-1) so in reality we were being issued

all sorts of goodies that we couldn't wear with the military uniform.

As the temperatures plummeted recently, people started to wear the fleece pullover, over the military uniform. Someone at division wrote a letter stating that this was OK, even though its not written anywhere. Well many people wore the garment as they desired and then the corps sergeant major came over to the division headquarters. The corps sergeant major is a senior enlisted man who out ranks on paper all the other enlisted people for the III Corps or in other words, he is the highest ranking enlisted soldier in all of middle east for the US military. He was screaming at all the soldiers to get those black fleece jackets

off because they were out of uniform and they were not in the regulations.

He was belittling everyone, both officers and enlisted alike. Several high ranking enlisted soldiers got into a good verbal row with him over it, but they lost and so everyone took their black fleece pullovers off. Many thought of writing letters to editors about how much the taxpayers had spent on these beautiful fleece jackets and were completely unable to wear. Many of us talked

61

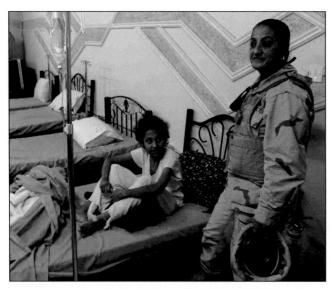

No other story gripped the readers on the e-mail list like Hara's story. (See November 17th entry) The little girl was out playing when an IED exploded burning most of her lower body.

about how an old guy such as the sergeant major who had nothing better to do than to go around and throw temper tantrums over what people were wearing should just get out of the military all together. There was a whole lot of "Oh yeah says you" and "there's that ol' messed up army again, issues soldiers the best equipment in the world and won't let us use it."

Many of you are asking, doesn't an officer outrank a senior enlisted soldier. The answer is yes, but you must exercise that authority wisely lest you bring great discredit upon yourself. It's all very political in the military once you get above squad level and the politics grow the higher in echelons and rank that you go. The commanding general, Major General Chiarelli went over or called over and really got into it with him and the next morning Chiarelli announced on the division radio frequency that all 1st Cavalry Division soldiers will wear the black fleece pullover if they so desire and no one, absolutely no one that doesn't outrank a two-star general will tell them no they cannot.

Thanks to the taxpayers, a heated election year and a commanding general with an Italian temper, we are all very warm and snug as we go about our business now.
God bless us, God bless us everyone.

December 02, 2004

I said to some of you that I was going to try and get into the holiday spirit by buying, wrapping and sending gifts to some select few. I did what I said and all I have to say is that it did not help me to get into the Christmas spirit at all. I was so flustered with the shopping at the Iraqi bazaar.

My plan fell apart when I took all the stuff and packing

Diana proved invaluable to the Civil Affairs Section. Here she is visiting with Hara's relative at the home that Hara had not seen in many weeks due to being hospitalized at various clinics.

The translator Diana and army doctor, Captain Beuhner work together to put Hara into a Humvee for the trip to the Iraqi hospital. Her legs are bent around some braces because her charred skin shrank and would not flex enough to straighten her legs. The girl was unable to stand or walk on otherwise healthy legs.

material to the post office to be inspected prior to shipping it all off. Everything has to be inspected to make sure that we are not sending bad stuff home. The postal workers were so helpful that as I brought the second load of stuff in, they had already inspected, boxed and taped shut the first load.

I didn't have the chance to wrap at all. There was not even the opportunity to write a letter and stick in the box. I was very hurried through the whole event and am sad to say that the entire experience was not the least bit Christmassy.

The whole thing with sending gifts home is not in the buying and shipping, it's in the getting it to the post office and inspected that is such a hassle that those on the other end should be grateful for that monumental effort. This hassle is much worse during the hot season as it involves much sweating and chafing.

Later that day I received a package from my friends Bruno and Marlys Deleau. It was great to receive so much chocolate and hot chocolate and chocolate bars and chocolate everything. Then that night, with hot cocoa and spiced apple cider, I felt the Christmas spirit.

It wasn't the giving of gifts that gets me into the Christmas spirit, it's the getting of Christmas gifts that gets me into the Christmas spirit. "Its the gift getting season Charlie Brown." Maybe things never change and it's good to get things just like a kid, or more likely, I just haven't grown up yet.

Above: Hara's baby brother became lost in Colonel Welch's Kevelar helmet. Below: Hara's older sister was enamored with the colonel. It is customary for the most eligible young girls in the Middle East and Asian cultures to be married off to older and distinguished men such as the colonel.

Hara's older sister hurried around the barren house to make a traditional breakfast for the colonel and myself. We felt awkward eating the breakfast that might have been the only meal this family had that day. The pita bread was really great. I was amazed that a family in humble means, in a war-torn country and in Baghdad of all places was able to obtain fresh baked bread, fresh jam and butter, really good tea and even modern diapers for the little one.

God bless us. God bless us everyone.

December 05, 2004

About the only thing I can write about tonight is the Iraqi National Guard (ING). There are some really great leaders in the ING and there are some truly courageous soldiers. I have been working with getting Iraqi media to cover the ING and so I have been privy to some inside information and insight.

Hara arrives at yet another hospital. The doctors at this hospital promised to operate starting immediately, but three months later they had only attempted a skin graft that had failed.

Lieutenant Colonel Welch first found Hara at one of the many hospital clinics that the Civil Affairs section was working with. He had to ask her about her problem and then he was unable to tear himself away from trying to help. The task of seeking medical attention for Hara in Baghdad was more than a formidable one. He is seen here playing with Hara's younger half brothers.

Today I saw some ING soldiers washing a vehicle that was shot a couple of times. Most of their vehicles that patrol the worst and most terrorist ridden streets are Toyota pickup trucks with machinegun mounts in the back. That is not a lot of armament if you ask me. Just about all of their Toyotas have bullet holes in them and some of them are just riddled with holes. It's amazing that these men keep going out on patrol in these things. It's also amazing that the recruitment still continues to go well in spite of all the threats and danger. My hat's off to these truly die-hard patriots.

There is mass corruption in the ING and the Iraqi police Service (IPS). The claims are true, but I am convinced that they are grossly embellished by the rumor mill in Baghdad.

The same rumor mill that Saddam Hussein helped create and use to his iron fisted control is the same rumor mill that has everyone believing that we the US are actually hiring people to carry out all these terrorist attacks so that we can justify staying here and continue stealing the oil. This same rumor mill has generated the mass belief that the IPS and the ING are massively corrupt.

I am amazed at the American military officers that scoff at what the rumor mill says about the US, readily jump on the band wagon with the same rumor mill when it comes to the belief about mass corruption in the IPS, ING and the new government.

In just one year, the Iraqi Security Forces, which is the summation of the army and the ING and the Iraqi police and other institutions, has come an enormous distance, but they still have a long way to go. Hope that gives you some insight. The pictures of the truck will be forthcoming and like everything else I

I just received word that I will be traveling to Qatar for a four day pass. With two days of travel it is actually a six day pass from this place.

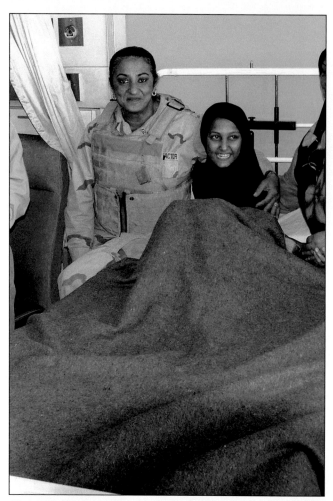

Above: Diana poses with Hara at her new hospital bed in the upper floors of Saddam Hussein's personal hospital. Below: The view from Hara's bed of central Baghdad, north of the Green Zone.

do, they will take a long time for me to get to you. "It's going to take some time."

___

December 11, 2004

Qatar is a small, very pro-US country south of Kuwait along the coast of the Persian Gulf. Soldiers go there for R&R and are allowed to drink three cheap American beers a day. I am not looking forward to being there, I am looking forward to not being here. It has been a hellish week here at Camp Al Tareer (Out-the-rear) as I call it. This is the new name for the camp and means liberty.

I have been receiving packages from various people and I have been hearing gossip that more are on the way. Thank you all for supporting your local soldier. I can't tell you how important it is to know that I am in your thoughts and your prayers.

___

December 13, 2004

I was able to go out and take pictures of up-armored vehicles while escorting two very interesting reporters from Europe. They are covering stories about the additional armor added to military vehicles by soldiers. That is to say they are covering the homemade "Mad Max" jury-rigging by the good ol' boys from the Louisiana National Guard.

I took a bunch of pictures while I was with them. We got some pretty good ones and I will be sharing them with you all. I think that this story depicting the homemade attempts to add protection has been a long time coming. The photographs you'll see are actually much better than the homemade attempts that my rotation had. The southern boys will survive, because they know how to weld a lot better than my group did. Of course I drove up the highway in a soft-skin Humvee with the plastic canvas doors.

Tomorrow I leave for Qatar and just in time. Robin Williams the famous comedian from "Mork and Mindy" will be coming tomorrow and he will be holding a press conference just 15 feet from where

Hillbilly Armor, as it was referred to, covers up a 5-Ton Army Truck.

I am sitting right now. Thank God I won't be here for that circus.

FOUR DAY PASS TO QATAR
December 14, 2004

You gotta love the military travel service. I spent all day yesterday from 8:00 in the morning until 10:00 last night waiting and flying and then really waiting for the bus and then really waiting for the gates to open. I am really happy to be here and not there (1st CAV).

This place is really dry and flat (surprise). I have signed up for two trips out on the town of Doha in this country called Qatar pronounced like guitar but with a K sound. One of the trips is an Arabian Safari in SUVs winding up at the beach for a Bar B' Que. The second trip is an outing to a really nice restaurant on the water.

I was able to have three drinks for the first time since Europe. Jack Daniels never

tasted so good.

December 15, 2004

Yesterday was a great day. I met up with a senior NCO who had an inside connection for everything that goes on around here so I hung out with her. I was able to go down to the big shopping mall that rivals any in the US and then we went down to the shopping district in downtown Doha.

Doha is the name of the city in Qatar. Soldiers are never allowed to go downtown and walk around and interact and such so this was a rare and unique opportunity. The shopping district is dominated with gold jewelry stores. I called this area Bling Bling Alley.

I can only take a few pictures here and there in Qatar as it's against the law because the terrorist threat is felt very much in this very wealthy country. Evidently many of the terrorists have their families live here in

Qatar and the Qatarian government pays them money not to cause trouble here in Qatar. That has been the policy for the whole Islamic region, capitulate and cooperate to get the terrorists off their back for today.

Evidently the old regime of sheiks held all the oil money for themselves. Their sons murdered them and took over the country for the purpose of setting up a distribution system for disseminating the oil money to the people. When a young man graduates from high school and comes of age he receives a lot of money. If he gets married, he receives a lot of money. If he graduates from college, he receives a lot of money. Kids bring more money.

The entire society is so laden with money that they don't have to work, so the nation brings in Filipinos to work the jobs. Now the population is more foreigners than Qatari. All this information and cultural awareness from just one visit to a shopping mall.

The country and the city of Doha are incredibly clean. This much I could easily see.

Today a bunch of us are going on an official trip to a fancy restaurant down on the waterfront. I am looking forward to this dining experience. Tomorrow I am going on the Arabian Safari.

December 17, 2004

Qatar is a country down the coast of the Persian Gulf and lies due east from Saudi Arabia. The city in Qatar is called Doha and holds almost the entire country's population, somewhere around 750,000. Many refugees from around the Arab region relocate to Qatar for which they are at some point, put on the payroll from the oil.

Many of us went on a Arabian Safari which was a four wheel drive trip through the sand dunes. I was told that this Arabian Safari as they are called are a major tourist attraction and the drivers are often Palestinian and

This vehicle is the Army's new 5-Ton and has been up-armored by the soldiers. These newer vehicles were known to have problems with the fatiguing of metal due to the increased weight of the add-on armor causing the cab to become separated from the chasis or even fall off of the moving vehicle in one reported case.

make about $17,000 a month between their money from the oil fields and their wages from driving SUVs.

The foreign workers who stay, at some point will receive a plot of land of about 800 square meters.

With regard to the Safari, we all piled into cramped Landcruisers and Nissan SUVs. We drove for an hour to the sand dunes and then drove around there for about 2.5 hours.

We ended up at the beach site where we had a kabob bar b' que. We also went swimming in the Persian Gulf. The water was extremely salty and we were able to float better there than in regular pool water. It was a beautiful day. That was a great day.

It was not until I was floating in the waves did I realize that I was on a vacation type break from Baghdad. Everyone had similar comments that if we had not taken the Safari, then we would never have know that it was a four day pass.

Most people would just like to be given four days off without being disturbed right here and I believe that they would get much more rest than the trip to Qatar, but it is impossible for anyone to be left alone.

I was able to see the traditional Arabian fishing boats, now without the mast and sails and more for pleasure than for fishing.

On the last day we got up at 3:00 am in the morning and started the hurry up and wait process in getting back to Baghdad. Here I am.

December 19, 2004

I couldn't sleep one morning so I got up and I found some incredible colors in the sky. I grabbed my good camera and snapped off about 30 photos. The pictures are almost the real colors, but the shutter speed was sped up to 140 to 180th of a second, which made the photos darker than what I was really looking at. There were some soldiers doing PT so I captured a couple of them on bytes.

A much more common form of Hillbilly Armor was simply putting some steel plating over the doors such as in the case above.

December 22, 2004

For those of you who have been caught up in the "lack of up-armor kits for Humvees" let me tell you about some heroes I have come across: the Iraqi National Guardsmen (ING).

The ING was originally called the ICDC or the Iraqi Civil Defense Corps. The US wanted to change their image and their real-world credibility so their name was changed to ING during a campaign to rid the insurgents from the ranks. The name change and policy changes in recruitment have put the ING on the right track towards a more structured and formidable force.

The new recruits have to go through a semi-rigorous 12 days of basic training before they are linked up with their units and their squads and begin patrolling the streets of Baghdad.

The vehicle that their squad patrols around in is usually a Nissan mini pickup truck with a crew served machinegun mounted on a pedestal in the rear. Two other riflemen with AK 47s will ride in the back with the machinegunner and point their weapons one third off to either side of the primary direction of the main gun. This causes a weapon and pair of eyes to be focused in every direction to return fire, not if, but when they are attacked.

They are absolutely certain to be attacked sometime in their military career. For their service they receive about $100 in Iraqi Dinar. This will pay for about 1/4 of a months rent for a small apartment in a bad neighborhood.

I personally witnessed that most of the vehicles at the

Bling Alley in Doha, Qatar was an interesting place. This was the only time that I was able to walk around in civilian clothes and shake hands with true Arab people as if I were a tourist. Soldiers call this Bling Alley because of all the cheap gold jewelry shops highlighted with bright neon lights and fancy signs. Every major Arab city has a "Bling Alley" District that appeals to the local shopping culture.

The camp site for the Bar B' Que right next to the Persian Gulf where soldiers were entertained to traditional Arabian cuisine and were able to play volleyball and even ski down the sand dunes on the alpine skis seen in the foreground. It was not until I was floating up and down on the waves in the Persian Gulf that I was truly able to realize that I was away from Baghdad.

brigade headquarters had at least several bullet holes in them. If the American soldiers were ordered to patrol the streets of Baghdad under such conditions they would probably throw down their weapons and move to Canada and vote Democrat for the rest of their lives.

Conversely I believe that if Americans were told to defend America under such conditions, they likewise would be lined up for city blocks waiting to enlist.

The Iraqi military surgeon stated this week that his staff has screened 3,800 Iraqi police recruits this month alone.

If their neighbors find out that they are members of the ING, they will receive death threats that are very real. If their identity and association with the Iraqi Security Forces (ISF) is found out, but the insurgents are unable to find where they are living as most of them are living from house to house and

relative to relative, then a cousin or mother receives the death threat if they do not cooperate in turning the ISF member in to be captured.

I was absolutely amazed to see how the soldiers patrolled the streets of

Baghdad in these homemade gun-trucks.

I had the opportunity to talk to some ING officers and they too go out on these patrols. They talked about how some of the new incoming officers were so scared to go out on the patrol that they were shaking with fear. They talked about what cowards they were and how they are now treating them like cowards. I thought to myself about all the whining and moaning going on in the US military while they were describing this to me.

I was humbled by the courage that these men display everyday in this horrible situation that we, the American military carrying out the orders of the US government, have created by forcing on the Iraqi people our intent for a new democratic government with an Iraqi military that is being forced to stand up in the face of terrorist warfare, the type and scale the world has

Soldiers from all over Iraq rest from the hot sun inside a traditional Arabian tent. The colorful canvas is typical for the Arabic style of decor. The rugs that the soldiers are sitting on are true hand made Arabic and Persian rugs. Yes the rugs were put directly on the sand and yes the soldiers were required to take their shoes off when they went in.

A favorite for soldiers is the Arabian Safari in SUV's in the Sand Dunes National Park along the Persian Gulf. This is a shot looking down a steep slope at the tidal flats below and the vehicles ahead.

Soldiers visit at the Bar B' Que site next to the Persian Gulf.

Looking up the same steep slope as the previous picture at the last SUV coming down.

never seen before.

I'd like to quote Major General Chiarelli, the 1st Cavalry Division Commander when he was talking to a high level translator in the Green Zone one day. "I am absolutely amazed at the incredible acts of heroism that I hear about every week. Iraq does not lack for patriots and courage at all."

I realize that I am biased on these matters because I earnestly believed in what the US has been doing all along and I have sown a great deal of my life into this effort along with all the other soldiers around me. I also am fully aware of the corruption and the great distance that the ING must go to, to be able to handle the

responsibility for security in this nation.

As I contemplate the political infighting of the Division Main and even within my own National Guard unit and think back on the quibbling and whining to include my own sniveling, I am very humbled by what the young men of the ING are accomplishing day in and day out.

Their true basic training is the warfare that they are fighting in and when all is said and done this country will have a military that is capable of fighting very well. The Iraqi society will be filled with many heroes in every capacity as they are truly national guardsman and will leave service for the work force when the country

is stabilized.

I am perhaps overly optimistic about the future potential for this country because I want to believe that what we are doing is so necessary and justifiable. These points need to be considered at least in contemplating the possible and probable future of Iraq.

———————————

December 24, 2004

Merry Christmas everyone;

It's a busy night tonight with the big explosion in downtown Baghdad with

many Iraqi people dead and injured. The phone is ringing off the hook with media wanting facts and information and the colonel is in one of his pouty moods so nobody wants to really talk to him.

Last year at this time, Kevin and I were on top of his roof working until 2:00 in the morning repairing the roof and racing the clock. We finished cleaning up about 4:00 in the morning. I remembered asking myself "how did I end up here in this predicament?" Now this year I am here in Baghdad Iraq working Christmas eve on the night shift covering

A favorite part of the four day pass was the four-wheeling in SUVs. The driver here of the vehicle poses with some of the soldiers who rode in his vehicle. It amazed many of us that we came from Iraq and here we were putting our lives into the hands of an Arab as he raced along the sand dunes. Many of the drivers were actually Palestinian immigrants.

The day of four-wheeling and Bar b' Que ended with a short bon-fire. The local company, hired to do these 'Desert Safaris", packed so much into one day the soldiers were exhausted, by the time the fire was done most were ready to sleep the entire two hour drive back to Doha.

all the media actions about a major explosion in this country on the other side of the planet and I'm asking myself "how did I end up here in this predicament?"

One thing is for sure. I need to plan my future Christmases out a lot better. I hope all of you are able to enjoy your Christmas without worry, without fear or concern and with your loved ones.

_____

December 29, 2004

Some thoughts on the latest Bin Laden tape. The video taped speech was mostly a cry to Jihad and a staunch calling to unite and fight off not only the Great Satan, but

When Santa's elves go bad they have to go to Baghdad, Iraq. This was a civilian contractor who got caught up in the Christmas Spirit.

Below: Moving Day. The day finally came when we had to pack our 20 foot container up and send it back to home station. Here all the gear is laid out ready for inspection. It took six months to be reunited with my personal belongings after this photo was taken.

also the new fledgling Iraqi government.

Usama Bin Laden really screwed up on this one. I don't see it getting lots of air time with Al Jazzeera and for good reason. Bin Laden made two crucial mistakes. He called on the Iraqi Muslims to attack infrastructure and told them to unite with Abu Musab Zarqawi who is the person in charge of Al Qaeda operations in Iraq.

The first mistake calling Iraqi Muslims to attack infrastructure as a form of stopping the progress of a new democratic sovereign nation was really a call for the Iraqi people to make themselves poorer and more miserable.

There is a real problem with no electricity and no heat during the winter months. The Iraqi people as

69

a whole are really getting fed up with the nonsense of this war on terrorism happening in their neighborhood. The huge reduction in standard of living, basic necessities and utilities has made their lives miserable and a call to expand on this, really united the Iraqis against Al-Qaeda and for the new Iraq.

Bin Laden had almost no following at all in Iraq and still does not, but what following he does have is mostly non-religious Sunni who want to keep Iraq destabilized so that they can retake control of Iraq after the US gets tired and leaves. These people are losing their base support due to the miserable conditions in Iraq caused by prolonged resistance.

I believe that Usama Bin Laden lost a lot of support and the connectivity from what little operating cooperation he had with some of the Sunni former regime loyalists. I further believe that he distanced himself from possible future support from the young people who want their electricity and fuel supply problems fixed.

The next mistake was where Bin Laden talked about his Lieutenant Zarqawi operating in Iraq, refutes the enormous disinformation that we have been trying to accomplish for months now: that is the normal Iraqi's belief that the US forces have made Zarqawi up as a fictitious character and that we are responsible for carrying out the terrorist attacks in order to keep the Iraqi people oppressed so we can justify staying here and continue to steal their oil.

When Bin Laden called on Muslims everywhere to unite with Zarqawi, he gave this person real credence as a real human being carrying out real attacks on his own and basically told the whole Arab region that the US military really has been telling the truth.

It is hard to tell how much influence this tape is going to have on the Arab people and what they believe, but it shows that Bin Laden is detached from the reality of Iraq and the problems that the US military is facing. He obviously does not know that most Iraqis didn't believe in Zarqawi and that they will be turned against him and his cause by the call to worsen their lives.

Just remember when reading these e-mails that I have been wrong before and could be again.

Above: Iraqi police control the streets in downtown Baghdad early in OIF II. A big step in standing up the Iraqi police was getting them to swarm an area after an IED attack so that the Iraqi people could see them making a show of force and taking control. This was one of the many big successes early on. Below: Oday worked with us at the Division-Main. When he first started working with the new Iraqi police force in 2003 under 1st Armored Division, he was asked to pose for a recruiting poster along with three others. They agreed under the auspices that the posters would only be on display at the military installations. The posters were circulated throughout all of Iraq and the foursome became famous overnight. Their lives were completely changed. They lived in fear of reprisal from anti-Iraqi forces. They were interviewed many times and appeared in many articles since the time the photograph was taken.

December 30, 2004
Tripping all over Baghdad

I thought I'd go on a little drive about around Baghdad just to see the sites and take a few pictures. The day turned out to be quite

driving through a nomadic type market street lined with tent type stands and very crowded during the rush hour of evening. We inched

SSG Gray along with the rest of the Shadow Force soldiers delivered AK-47s to the Facilities Protection Service (FPS) guards. The FPS was stood up along with the new Iraqi police and the Iraqi Civil Defense Corps in response to the looting that took place after the invasion. The guards were given a much more substantial role in the protection of key buildings and administrative institutions. The AK-47s along with some sniper rifles were clear indications that their responsibilities and authorities overlapped with that of police and the military. Many of these well armed security guards distinguished themselves during the uprising. Below: An FPS guard brought his family to work with him at one of the District Advisory Council (DAC) buildings, perhaps to protect them from threats.

an experience I don't think I'll ever forget. One of the most memorable events was

along the crowded streets with people waving, grimacing and soliciting us for

water and candy.

We later got caught up behind a severely damaged bridge over the Tigris River. It was the steel trestle kind about 60 feet off the water. A car bomb had blown a hole in the middle of the already narrow bridge. People pilfered a local rail road bed for the iron rails and laid them over the hole. Heavy traffic has been rumbling across the steel rails as they wobble back and forth because they were never fastened to the bridge itself. We also had to negotiate this and as I

A Light Armored Vehicle (LAV) was much more maneuverable than the Bradley Fighting Vehicles in downtown Baghdad.

walked across the rails I could see the Tigris River below. The Humvees did just fine as their large tires easily spread their weight across several rails at a time. The sergeant in charge of the convoy was up a head yelling at the Iraqi people to get their cars out of the way because so many of them had charged the oncoming lane with their vehicles because they simply didn't want to wait in line for their turn and they didn't care about following rules. When ever American soldiers show up in these mob type scenes, many Iraqis are grateful be-

cause we establish order where there has never been order before in such scenarios.

An example of this can readily be seen with the serious fuel crisis in Baghdad. There are enormous lines as the new Iraqi government tries to re-establish the socialist system of fuel distribution in Iraq where the fuel is subsidized ridiculously low to the consumer and mass corruption and gross incompetence results. There are usually mobs formed as people pay Iraqi policemen bribe money to let them

cut in line and such. Iraqis will always drive greater distances and wait up to 12 hours at a gas station where they know American soldiers are patrolling because they know that the corruption will not take place and that they will be treated well enough if they just wait their turn.

Such was the case here where Iraqi drivers unwilling to drive by the rules and unwilling to wait their turn had completely jammed up the only river crossing for many miles. Sergeant Gray came to the rescue and yelling in English and pointing his M-4 carbine weapon at

71

people while barking out English commands is the international language for "DO WHAT THE HELL YOU KNOW I WANT YOU TO DO!" It worked and those people that had rushed the oncoming lane backed their vehicles up and got out of the way and by that time the Humvees had maneuvered their way to the front of the line and we were out of this really weird situation that just sprang up on us out of nowhere. Soldiers are faced with the weirdest predicaments. I will never forget the way I felt and the intense excitement as I walked through the crowd of people there on the bridge. I am sorry to say that I did manage to forget my camera as I climbed out of the back of the Humvee so there are no pictures from that particular event.

January 25, 2005

For those of you who are religious, I will share the following true story.

Pray that I don't have to sleep on "Camel Poop"

The other day I reached a sorrowful prayerful moment when contemplating the month long stay in the tent that will probably leave me living off of 1-3 hours of sleep a day. This is no fun. I prayed that God would change the situation so that we could stay in our trailers until we leave.

Last night I called Dad and he shared this story with me. I'll write it from Dad's perspective.

I was at church on Sunday and one of the ladies of the church motioned me over to talk to her. She had a story she wanted to share with me so we went to the back of the church. She told me that she took her 10 yr old boy

Originally called the Iraqi Civil Defense Corps, the ICDC name was changed to the Iraqi National Guard (ING) to help improve the image. The volunteer soldiers received 12 days of basic training and and a small Japanese truck to go fight the insurgency with.

Every ING truck I saw had bullet holes in them. This one had the fewest bullet holes at the time so it was chosen to be the new Brigade Commander's vehicle. The driver who was shot from this incident actually got away with minor injuries. The holes on the other side of the vehicle caused severe injuries to the passenger.

The ING trucks had pedestals mounted in the back in which a heavy machinegun was mounted and the gunner sat in the seat behind the machinegun.

to the library to find a book and the boy found a book on poop that caught his attention and he wanted to read about poop. (Now keep in mind that during the 2.5 yrs I worked on my M.S. at WSU I had to spend a significant amount of time looking at bug poop under microscope). It isn't just young boys who are fascinated with poop these days.

He was reading about poop when he came to the chapter of the history of poop. The text explained how Arabs would gather camel poop into a pile during the winter months and sleep on it to stay warm (decomposing organic matter gives off heat as it degrades).

The boy read this and immediately demanded to pray for the son of that man who stands up in front of the church and leads singing. "His son is in Iraq and we need to pray for him so that he doesn't have to sleep on camel poop" the young boy demanded. And so this boy named Josh and his mother stopped what they were doing and prayed that Tim who is all the way on the other side of the planet would not have to sleep on camel poop.

Well Dad shared this story with me and it all clicked in my head. For those of you who believe, this boy's prayer was in response to my despair for the upcoming month in a crowded tent sleeping on what is now a very muddy floor. Camel poop to sleeping on a cot in a small crowded tent with a dirt floor is a bit of a stretch, but I was greatly encouraged by this story and it's timeliness. For those of you believe you can now pray that CPT Tate and his compadres don't have to sleep on camel poop, and can instead sleep in their trailers until we leave.

Hope you enjoyed the little

Four members from the National Guard that bravely worked, lived and fought with the Iraqi National Guard along the Haifa Street area in downtown Baghdad. These soldiers were with Sergeant Damien Ficek when he was killed in action. Sergeant Damien Ficek was from my Alma Matter, Washington State University, and we had a mutual friend in one of the professors. This was the closest contact I had with anyone who died in action, even though it was my job to report all casualties for the first four months of the deployment during the height of the uprisings.

story of encouragement.

_____

January 26, 2005

The pictures are gone, but the rhetoric lives on. Long live the rhetoric. Tonight's topic: right-wingers digging for dirt on Kerry discredits all of the right-wing.

Senator John Kerry came and visited the troops here in Iraq and he blessed the 1st Cav Division with his presence and he actually walked about eight feet from where I now type out this letter enlightening you as to what is going on in the world. This being the public affairs office, there were plenty of people around with cameras and one of our outstanding soldiers, a Private First Class Charles Maib took the official photos of the Senators visit for the military and his photos went out in the official news release. The

news media picked up on the photos and they were seen everywhere. CNN and AP

were some of the biggies. Private Maib was in no doubt flattered and while searching

for his name in lights or in the by-lines he found several web sites using his photos in a discrediting manner.

The photos were sent out completely undoctored in anyway, but there has been much speculation by conservative groups with agendas against Senator Kerry as to digital manipulation of photographs. Many people have looked at this picture and seen the half nub of a finger of a young female soldier and responded with a conspiracy theory that she is flipping him off and the full length of the finger was airbrushed out. This has been spun into a coercion conspiracy theory by many that reason that the Senator had the soldiers ordered to stand around him and listen to him and pretend to be glad he was here. Some have said that PFC Maib must be a fictitious character the army made up to keep from having any real soldier held accountable for this fraudulent photo.

PFC Maib has become

Corpral Bliss from the Bay area displays the bracelet with SGT Ficek's name. Sergeant Damien Ficek you are not forgotten.

quite upset at the irrational response from these right-wingers with agendas. These people are clearly digging and digging into a photograph that was taken half way around the world making up ridiculous interpretations, inferences and theories behind the juxtaposition of a young soldiers knuckle. The stories and conspiracies that have been conjured up similarly to witches standing around a boiling cauldron conjuring up spirits, are unfortunately becoming more and more common among the conservative right wing and bring great discredit upon not only the cackling conjurers, but also on the entire right-wing to include the Republican party as well. When you're right you don't need to make stuff up like this.

Should conservatives be self disciplining as a group on these people as well as all those who, for one reason or another, represent the gun totin' righteous right-wingers. This would mean silencing many conservative

The hardest thing about military service is the good-byes. This is one of the farewells I was dreading. I gave each soldier from the Shadow Force a coin from the unit I came with and it made for an emotional event for all of us. I still keep in touch via e-mail with some of them. I hope that this project will some how bring us all back together again.

Below: Lieutenant Aubin not only served with me in Baghdad, not only is a fellow WSU alumnus, but also was a fellow student with me in the Geology Department. During our studies he, at the time a proud Buck Sergeant swore up and down that he would never become an officer. Never say Never. Notice the mulitple bracelets.

talk show hosts around the United States and thus violate that ever important right to free speech. How far can an institution go before wise discipline turns into depriving of fundamental rights? How much control and discipline can an entire movement of institutions and masses, such as the right or left wing exercise over the individuals before "Big Brother is Watching?"

You know. I probably don't have anyone still reading at this point without the pictures. I should just shut up and get back to work. The real lesson behind all of this is that we, the glorious night shift crusaders were astounded at something so simple as a photograph that Private Maib who is now sitting right here in front of me as I write, has been misconstrued and blown out of proportion by people with too much time on their hands and who listen to conservative talk radio a liiiiiiittle toooooooo much.

That's all I really wanted to say and look at how much verbosity it took to get the point across. For those of you who don't know me, I talks as good and as much as I rites.

_____

January 29, 2005

Well this is it, again. I would like to convey my gratitude for all your support through this time one more time. I will be keeping in touch from time to time, but please don't be alarmed when the peppering of e-mails from this account

stops. I'm OK Dad. Don't call the Department of Defense looking for me or send out an all points bulletin.

One last comment with a fool hearted prediction. I'm so sorry but I just couldn't resist to put my foot in my mouth one more time. I'm just so weak in this area, particularly with a closed audience. There are many predictions going around as the results of the elections. Here's mine. The Kurds will walk away with the majority party lead and thus choose a Kurdish Prime minister. The Kurds are all united and in a much safer region where candidates are allowed to campaign and talk to the people much more than in the Baghdad area.

The Sunni are obviously going to have a tougher time getting both the numbers and their votes focused on anyone of their many political parties. The Shia are all over the spectrum. They alone account for over 100 parties. There is very little campaigning going on in the Sunni region and even less going on in the Baghdad area. The ballot will contain 111 parties, some without names. The

The trip home took an entire week. The beginning of the hurry up and wait started in the military air terminals where soldiers had to find ways to entertain themselves for days while waiting to fly.

Kurds have the most cohesive and well organized political movement inside the most stabilized part of Iraq. I think that they stand a good chance to have one of their parties take the most votes of all. With the way the Shia fight, they may never get enough voting power focused on any one party to get a majority lead in the parliaments.

Of course if I'm wrong, then I will again be embarrassed by my "hoof in mouth" disease that I have suffered from so badly during this tour of duty.

_____

January 30, 2005

Ohhh those egg sucking liberal media types

The closer you get to home, the nicer the seats get and the nicer the interior design gets.

The election is over and it was a stunning victory for the Iraqi people and a devastating defeat for the insurgents. The whole world knows that the insurgents don't have the where-with-all to carry out their threats. The networks, who just days ago were trying to hype up speculated measurable marks of success for the elections, have said very little about the percentage of turnout. The word here in the Task Force Baghdad puzzle palace is in the neighborhood of 70% turnout for the city of Baghdad.

Christian Amanpour of CNN was told this number in person by the commanding general and she referred to the topic as too difficult to assess at this time. She lied through her Iranian lips to the world and without remorse.

We had a lot of incoming today while I was trying to sleep and one of the rockets landed close enough to wake me up. I felt the shock wave through the bed in my room. That rocket was close and big. Nobody was hurt as the rocket landed in an open area between life support areas (LSA, but really means trailer courts).

_____

February 03, 2005

Thanks to Josh I am not sleeping on Camel Poop... Yet.

And there was waiting and waiting on the inside of buildings and waiting on the outside of buildings and waiting while seated and waiting while standing.

I have had no trouble at all finding friends here that are staying and are more than happy to let me sleep on their floor. So much that I was able to be picky and choosy and am staying in a room where I have a key and my own bed. If this falls through, I already have backups in the works. This is a very good reason to make every opportunity to develop good working relations with absolutely everyone of all ranks.

There are many people here, both on active duty and from the reserves who did not go out of their way to establish good working relationships and maintain them throughout the year not thinking that it would do them any good, and now are regretting it as they have to commute from work to the tents where they have a below average sleeping environment. Many of those commuting have been discussing the problems and challenges that they have to face. Ahh the benefits of being a nice guy.

Please don't send any more packages after today.

We had our 20 foot container inspected-loaded-locked and sealed the other day. That was the single biggest headache of the entire redeployment process for us. It feels good to have that out of our hair.

_____

February 13, 2005

I see many changes for the better over this past year. When we first got here in March, everyone was watching the Mehdi militia of Sadr City and the Former Regime Extremists (FRE). There was a potential powder keg that could have and eventually did explode.

Instead of fighting the blast all at once and killing many innocent bystanders, and consequently turning many fence sitters against us, the decision makers chose to fight a long drawn out surgical battle on both fronts which wore not only the enemy out, but wore the public out as well and turned many of the fence sitters into informants to get the fighting over with.

That powder keg potential no longer exists thanks to the 1st Cavalry and the 1st Marine Divisions. I once criticized the decision makers, and in retrospect I now praise them.

There were many infrastructure improvements that were cut down, literally in the form of nine blown up power transmission line towers that crippled the city's electrical power. The socialist fuel distribution system that the local government insisted on carrying over from the old regime, combined with mass corruption, has crippled the city's ability to drive and heat with oil.

I once believed that communism could succeed in limited conditions such as a small island nation with a homogeneous population base, but now after being in Iraq I see the error of my ways. The Iraqi government needs to promote capitalism at the fuel pump. I will never complain about the ever greedy profiteering oil companies again. The alternative is much worse I assure you.

The reporters are saying the insurgents have stepped up attacks since the elections. I am telling you that in the grand scheme of things that is absolutely false. The attacks are fewer overall and they are less potent comparing those occurring after the elections with the three months leading up to the elections. The combination of US soldiers and more

And then when you get back to Ft. Lewis where the journey began, you get to wait standing up. This was really torment as we now had to wait standing up while staring at our loved ones in the bleachers.

importantly the increased Iraqi defense forces really cut down on attacks.

The organized crime that used to operate overtly is now having to hide for the first time. Too many Iraqi citizens are calling in and

Here I am with both my parents. The happy reunion pictures were taken by my older brother.

reporting crime and insurgency. We have a long way to go, but we have now come a long way as well.

This is a good, albeit long, article and as long as you keep a more optimistic view than the reporter writing it. I think you can get a pretty good gist of life in Baghdad and the burned out feelings of the soldiers who have

touched off the powder keg and fought the fire as they prepare to leave Baghdad. These soldiers, like myself, will never be the same person that came to Baghdad nearly a year ago.

_____

February 18, 2005

I'm now in the home stretch with less than four days left in Baghdad. So many thoughts are running through my head and so many emotions about all that has happened.

I am struggling to look forward to getting home.

There seems to be a weird mind game going on with the anticipation of returning both to the states and to Pullman. Its funny how these major life changes, even when clearly positive can bring great stress on us and emotional distress.

Even with that said, this tour of duty has been an absolute dream for me. I have not experienced the emotional distress of the oncoming mobilization, deployment and tour of duty that everyone else has faced. I originally shrugged off this lack of stress and emotional pressure as due to the carefree bachelor life I live, but it has become clear to me that the stressors from other life changing events over the last 15 years has clearly exercised my ability to adapt and overcome any changing environment.

More importantly I can see that I have been held aloft by the prayers and support from home. I thank you all for this very much. God has clearly been holding me up through all this.

At no time have I heard a single soldier ask why we're here and what on earth we're trying to accomplish. Everyone knew from their first day in Baghdad, if not from all the command briefings, then from the grateful looks on the Iraqi people that one sees each and every time they leave the wire. One smiling Iraqi child waving at a convoy passing by erases all doubts as to "what the mission is and why."

A special thanks goes out to Josh of La Pine, Oregon whose support prayers have kept ol' Captain Tate from sleeping in "Camel Poop." This term references an earlier e-mail in which sleeping on Camel Poop is likened to sleeping on a cot in a crowded tent during the day when people are coming and going. As it stands right now I am sleeping in a much nicer room with a bathroom and shower in the trailer. I will not have to sleep on Camel poop at all as originally ordered. Josh; Man I owe you. When I come to La Pine Oregon I'll have to take you out to your favorite burger and ice cream place.

As it now stands, I will get up from sleeping late Monday night on the 21st, go do the night shift till 8:00 Tuesday morning, take all my gear and rifle over to the temporary tent city where all my counterparts have been

sleeping on "Camel Poop" and wait there all day for a formation to tell us when on Wednesday our plane leaves for Kuwait.

We will fly to Kuwait sometime on Wednesday and then be bussed to a military installation where we will go through more out-processing. We will then go to the airport sometime late Thursday night where we will wait some more and then go through the mother of all customs inspections to include every envelope being opened, every pocket of every garment to include the one each and every soldier is wearing will be hand searched by the military customs police.

We will then wait some more and then board the plane where we will wait

some more. We will probably fly to Europe and have a four to six hour layover. We will not be allowed to go anywhere, just waiting there on the plane or in the military terminal. We will then fly maybe straight to McChord Air Force Base or maybe another layover on the east coast of America where we will wait some more. When the plane arrives in the Seattle area, probably sometime on Saturday morning, I will have been in the state of traveling for four complete days.

The army's hurry up and wait has not changed at all. I am not complaining because most soldiers will have to spend two weeks in Kuwait before they fly home. I expect this traveling time to be a challenge for me

personally. After we arrive home we have four hours of weapons turn in and paper work before we're allowed to do the warm and fuzzy reunion scene that you all get to see on TV.

I will try and take some pictures through all of this so I can have a complete photo album of this deployment from start to finish. I might send a few handfuls of photos on the same distro-list for the sole purpose of bringing the e-mail that I have been doing to a "full-circle" completion, if you will. God bless and thank you all for all your support.

And then the waiting was over with. Here I am hugging my dad. This was the first moment I had ever seen my father cry, and he sobbed. It was really difficult for me to deal with as it was for all my siblings who also showed up to greet me.

February 21, 2005
Last Day from Baghdad

This is it, the last night of work. By this time tomorrow I should be on a C-130 heading to Kuwait. It is unlikely that if things go well that I will be able to e-mail from this part of the world again. Many emotions and many thoughts reflecting on my year here in Iraq have been racing through my head these past few days.

A reoccurring theme keeps reminding me of the fact that I was here when history was being made. One of the most pivotal times in history has been made here in the Middle East over the past three years, and I was here in Baghdad, the hub of the Arab region when the greatest changes occurred. I really am proud that I served with the 1st CAV Division.

I am convinced that the soldiers did great as a whole. Sadr City and the Mehdi militia, Falluja, An Najaf, and the Sunni anti-Iraqi attacks would have sent most countries running and they did send many countries running. The powder keg of explosive potential has been detonated and we are still here. These colors did not run. Now beam me up Scotty!

I have spent a lot of time reflecting on what I did and what I could have done better. I am also examining where I can go

from here and what I want to do when I get back. I am looking forward to the traveling and rest.

I am looking forward to seeing you all again. Pray for safe travel and that the jam-ups at the airports would

Postscript

notes: I returned with my oldest sister Cheryl Hay to her home after the ceremony. My sister had remodeled her house, with kids having

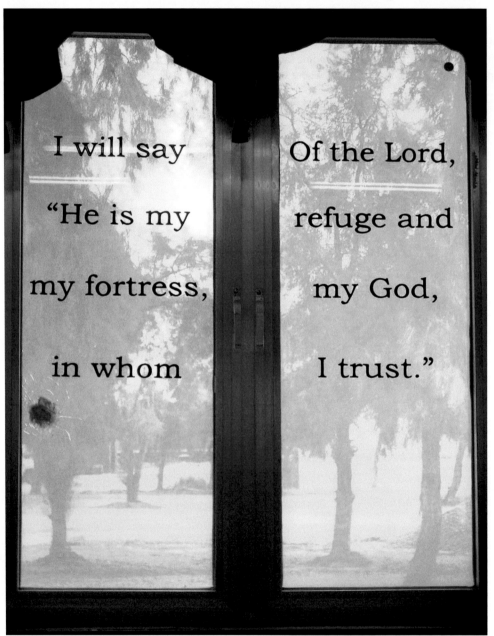

The 91st Psalm was divided up and written on all the windows of the chapel there at Victory North. The window with the passage "I will say of the Lord, He is my refuge and my fortress, my God, in whom I trust." was written on this window. Note the spider cracking in the lower left that looks like a baseball hit the window. A large rocket, probably the 120mm Chinese made silkworm rocket impacted outside in the grove of trees while the Lutheran service was going on inside the chapel. The blast threw debris in all directions. The explosion was the kind that makes the ground go down as the shock wave travels out from the blast. Debris, probably a rock was thrown at the chapel from the blast and impacted the window, but not enough to break the window. Church service continued.

clear up so we can get out of here on time.

_____

that I would have to sleep in the den. There, on my first night back from a year long deployment to Iraq, in the height of the war…..
in Edmonds, Washington, one of the most affluent suburbs of Seattle, my dear, dear, dear sweet sister had borrowed from a neighbor….. a US Army cot for me to sleep on……

Camel Poop!

gone and the one remaining guest room went to my parents. She informed me

Printed in the United States
By Bookmasters